GUIDE TO

PORTFOLIO MANAGEMENT

An investment philosophy

■

Clifford G. Dow, Sr.

CFA, CFP®, ChFC

Chief Investment Officer, Dow Wealth Management, LLC

DOW PUBLISHING COMPANY, INC.

Published by

Dow Publishing Company, Inc.
358 US Route One
Falmouth, ME 04105

Guide to Portfolio Management: An investment philosophy, 1st Edition

For information please contact:
Dow Publishing Company, Inc., 358 US Route One, Falmouth, ME 04105. 1.800.956.1435.

Published in the United State of America.

ISBN 978-0-615-23025-2

Library of Congress Control Number: 2008910308   DW2/DWB0081b

CONTENTS

DEDICATION

This book is dedicated to my beloved wife, Barbara Ann,
who assisted in its research,
and also patiently raised our four sons.

INTRODUCTION

In trying to pedal my wares as an investment broker some three and one half decades ago, I emphasized to a prospect my belief that he might accept investment information from myself, as a second broker, because, "in this business, we cannot get too much information." "Wrong," my prospect replied. "There is no shortage of information. It is what we do with the information that we already have that counts." My own modus operandi has been different ever since.

As esoteric as are many of the approaches to portfolio management that have emerged in recent years, it is, furthermore, astonishing how unsuccessful most of them have been. It is as though each new drug produced by the pharmaceutical industry were shortening, rather than lengthening, man's life expectancy.

These observations should be a source of comfort to the student of investing. Investment success appears to depend, not upon the amount or complexity of what we know, but rather upon how well we know, understand, believe, and apply the basics. In other words, there is light at the end of the tunnel, even before we enter the tunnel. We are closer than we may think to knowing all we need to know to be fully as successful an investor as any of the so-called "professionals" we might otherwise erroneously envy.

Every discipline has its unique nomenclature and tools. These accouterments are to one's craft, as the language and techniques of algebra are to the world of mathematics. For those practicing a trade, they are vital; for those seeking to understand the trade, they are similarly valuable. It is our purpose here to make you more comfortable with the language and tools of investing.

The information and concepts presented in this book should be useful, both to those with a limited familiarity with investing and to those with extensive investment knowledge and experience. For those of you in the former group, the sledding may be more difficult at times. Please persist, nevertheless.

Our approach is to immerse you in the complexities of the body of knowledge of investing at the outset. After repeated exposures to the same jargon and concepts, conversance with the subject matter will be achieved by osmosis, if in no other way.

— Clifford G. Dow, Sr.

1

INVESTING VERSUS GAMBLING

Some people regard investing as gambling; others, who think they are investing, are, in fact, gambling. The purpose of this chapter is to try to help the reader figure out to what extent he may be doing or contemplating either and, thereby, enable him better to allocate his financial assets in accordance with his true needs, objectives, and aspirations.

The following table of contents is included to serve as a summary, guide, and reference:

Practice

THE TRADITIONAL NOTION OF THE RELATIONSHIP BETWEEN RISK AND RETURN

The traditional expected return trade-off is illustrated by the first of the two following graphs. It says simply that, to achieve higher rates of return, we must take on greater risk; and, conversely, if we take on greater risk, we should expect higher returns.

This traditional assumed relationship appears to fall short of describing reality in two important respects: (1) The horizontal axis is in need of a different label, and (2) the shape of the curve is not accurate.

The second or revised graph seems to represent the real world more correctly, and it should also be more useful in helping us decide how to deploy our savings.

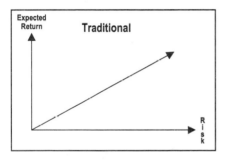

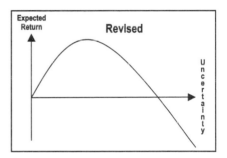

SEMANTIC PROBLEMS WITH THE WORD "RISK"

The difficulty with accepting the word "risk" as the parameter for the horizontal axis is its failure, in common parlance, to encompass the concept of pure "volatility," exclusive of the collateral issue of "safety."[1] The dimension of "risk," in the minds of most people, is a measure of *uncertainty* regarding the safety of one's principal and implies the possibility of a loss of some or all of that principal that is *permanent*. The word "volatility," on the other hand, implies *uncertainty* in the magnitude and/or timing of one's returns, at one extreme accompanied by the utmost stability of one's principal and, at the other extreme, accompanied by the possibility of a loss of principal that is only *temporary*.

Having money in the stock market is like riding a roller coaster. The "thrill" of the ride is a function of the "geometry" of the structure. This geometry, however, tells us nothing about the "safety" of the system. For knowledge of the safety of a roller coaster, we need data on the tolerance of its components to stress and its maintenance. We might use the term "volatility" to describe the "thrill" of the ride, and "risk" to discuss its "safety." The connotations of the word "risk," however, render the term inappropriate to embrace the "thrill" of a roller coaster ride, as removed from the issue of "safety."

By the same token, the term "risk," as typically used in discussing the securities markets, does not seem to encompass adequately the concept of "volatility" alone, as isolated from the concept of "safety." For that reason, the broader term, "uncertainty" has been substituted as the label for the horizontal axis on the revised expected return graph.

Perhaps the best example of the inadequacy of the term "risk" in describing the nature of a security is in the case of long-term U.S. Government bonds. On the one hand, long-term U.S. Government bonds are very volatile, with their prices fluctuating up and down violently with changes in the level of interest rates; on the other hand, U.S. Government bonds are regarded as the safest securities money can buy. Where, then, are long-term U.S. Government bonds to be located on the traditional risk-return graph? Hopefully, as will be explained next, the more inclusive word, "uncertainty," allows for a more appropriate placement.

THE HORIZONTAL AXIS — UNCERTAINTY

(From this point forward, it might be useful if the reader were occasionally to refer to the enhanced version of the revised expected return chart included as page 19.)

The horizontal axis on the revised chart depicts the relative degree of *uncertainty* in *both* the *magnitude* and *timing* of our returns and in the *safety* of our principal, for various ways we might deploy our money. As we move from left to right on the horizontal axis, we first encounter uncertainty in the sense of *volatility* in the *magnitude* of our returns. As uncertainty increases, it includes volatility in the *timing* of these returns; and, further on, up to the vertical dashed line, it includes the possibility of a *temporary* loss of our principal. The entire domain to the left of the vertical dashed line we call "investing." The salient characteristic of investing is the higher probability that any loss of principal we might experience will be only *temporary*.

As we proceed to the right of the vertical dashed line on the uncertainty continuum, we enter the domain of *risk* which involves a greater possibility of a *permanent* loss of our principal. Committing money in the domain of risk we call gambling.

THE VERTICAL AXIS — EXPECTED RETURN

The vertical axis represents "expected return." Expected return may be defined as the average rate of return for a large number of commitments to the same asset category over an extended period of time. In the case of common stocks, for example, the expected return is not for any specific common stock but, rather, is the average for the universe of common stocks of the same type over long periods of time.

It will be observed on the chart that, other than for the point of a zero rate of return, there are no other specific rates of return labeled on the vertical axis. Less erratic than *absolute* rates of return are *relative* rates of return, and less erratic than relative rates of return are *hierarchical* rates of return. The rates of return depicted on the chart are meant to be hierarchical and, for our purposes here, such a *hierarchy* should suffice.[2]

THE PARADOX OF THE EXPECTED RETURN GRAPH

As previously indicated, the traditional risk-return relationship implies that greater risk produces greater return. There is an ambiguity in this statement, however. Though higher risk may provide for the *possibility* of a *higher* return, it may also provide the *probability* of a *lower* return. If one of the consequences of taking incremental risk is the greater *probability* of a lower rate of return, we cannot legitimately contend that taking greater risk produces a greater return, even though that *possibility* may be there.

Capitalism does, however, seem to say that, if we are willing to subject our capital to greater volatility (greater uncertainty in the *magnitude* and *timing* of our returns and a greater probability that we may experience a *temporary* loss), we are entitled to a higher rate of return for our pain and suffering. Historically, capitalism has delivered such higher returns as compensation for such discomfort. It is, then, fair to say that there appears to be a strong positive correlation between *volatility* and return. The more volatility we are willing to accept in our investments, the higher return we should be able to earn on them.

THE PEAK AND DOWNWARD SLOPE IN THE REVISED GRAPH

As noted above, with the traditional risk-return graph, as risk increases indefinitely on the horizontal axis, return rises indefinitely on the vertical axis. In reality, however, experience shows that, at some point on the horizontal axis of uncertainty, where *volatility* merges into *risk*, expected return peaks out and starts downward.

But, how can this be? How can an asset category that exposes us to greater volatility and risk, but also provides us with a *lower* expected return, even exist? Why do people put their money into such an asset? If they did not, the asset category could not endure. Why are people willing to accept a lower return on, or pay a premium to their true financial worth for, some financial assets? There are two factors that can help explain this counter-intuitive shape of the revised expected return graph.

THE "LOTTERY FACTOR" AND THE ENTERTAINMENT VALUE OF RISK

Assume that we have a dollar burning a hole in our pocket and we can choose between one of two lottery tickets. The first lottery affords us one chance in fifty of winning $100. The second lottery offers us one chance in two million of winning $1 million. Which ticket would we buy?

At least some, if not most, of us will choose Lottery #2. Winning $100 may make a little water cooler conversation, but winning $1 million could change our whole way of life.

Lottery #1, however, more nearly resembles an investment. The law of averages says that, if we buy fifty of these lottery tickets, we shall invest $50 and reap a return of $100. That is a 100% return on our money.

Conversely, if we buy two million tickets to Lottery #2, it will cost us $2 million, and the law of averages says we will win only $1 million and so experience a 50% loss.

Clearly, though Lottery #2 does not make a very good investment, it has something going for it. Let us call it an entertainment or excitement value, or the "lottery factor." Even after doing the arithmetic, many of us might opt for Lottery #2.

The proclivity of great numbers of people for buying horse race and lottery tickets and making other sorts of bets with their money, whereby they are almost guaranteed to be losers over the long-term, demonstrates that, for some assets (lottery and horse race tickets), people are willing to pay for a financial asset a price in excess of what they know the asset financially to be worth. In other words, they are willing to put money into an asset with an expected return that is less than they know they could get elsewhere and, in fact, perhaps an expected return they know to be negative. This, then, is the definition of gambling. The bona fide benefit that gambling may provide, that investing may not, however, is entertainment and excitement.

It should, then, be understandable that many people are willing to deploy their money in ways that are a blend of investing and entertainment. If one has the choice of purchasing one common stock with an expected return of 10% per year and another common stock with an expected return of 1% per year, but with the remote possibility of a 1000% return, it should not be surprising that many people, at least with some portion of their money, will elect to purchase the latter common stock.

What is of critical importance, however, is that people who want to "invest" their money, and do not want to sacrifice a part or all of their return or principal for "entertainment," understand to what extent they are truly "investing" and to what extent they are actually "gambling."

THE "CURRENT" RETURN VERSUS "TOTAL" RETURN FACTOR

A second explanation of why an asset category may have an expected return less than might be expected by virtue of the volatility and risk associated with it concerns the ratio of its "current" expected return to its "total" expected return.

"Current" return refers to the periodic dividend or interest income we derive from an asset. "Total" return refers to the sum (or difference) of this dividend or interest income and the capital appreciation (or depreciation) in the value of the investment over some period of time. Total return is generally accepted as the more useful measure of true return and expected return.

Because there may be some uncertainty as to whether we shall experience appreciation or depreciation in an asset, as well as uncertainty as to when it will come about, all other things being equal, most investors would prefer to receive all of their return on an investment as reliable periodic current income payments. For this reason, many investors are willing to accept a lower total return on an investment in exchange for less uncertainty as to *when* that return will be forthcoming. They are willing to accept a lower *total* return as long as a greater portion of that *total* return comes to them as *current* return.

As an example, zero coupon U.S. Government bonds yield more than U.S. Government bonds of the same maturity but with coupons. The explanation is that there is less uncertainty with a coupon bond than with a zero coupon bond as to *when* there will be a favorable return on the bonds. For the greater uncertainty of the zero coupon bond, investors require a higher rate of total return.

The same trade-off exists with common stocks. Collectively, for stocks of comparable quality, low dividend growth stocks return more than high dividend income stocks. The incremental return on growth stocks is simply the marketplace's compensation to the growth stock investor for his acceptance of the greater uncertainty in the timing of the greater part of his return.[3]

As a general rule, then, the greater the portion of *total* return that is represented by *current* return, the lower total return one should expect to earn on the asset.

NON-ECONOMIC, UNNECESSARY, OR AVOIDABLE RISK

It is useful to draw a distinction between *economic* and *non-economic* risks. Capitalism pays for the former but not for the latter. In the management of our financial assets, it is especially important to recognize those risks for which we will not be paid.

As an analogy, if, when we go to work in the morning, we must cross a street, we expose ourselves to the risk of being run over. This is a risk for which capitalism will pay us. If we cross the street and get to work, hopefully, we can do something productive; if we do not cross the street, we cannot get to work, and so we cannot be productive. In part, then, we are paid for taking the risk of crossing the street. This is an economic, necessary, and unavoidable risk, and so capitalism will pay us for taking it.

Increasing one's exposure to risk, however, does not necessarily assure a higher return. If, for example, before we enter the office in the morning, we decide to walk back and forth across the street a dozen times, though we will increase our exposure to risk, we will not increase our productivity nor increase the return on our day's endeavors. We have exposed ourselves to a non-economic, unnecessary, and avoidable risk.

In investing, the most common risk considered unnecessary, avoidable, and non-economic, and for which capitalism will not pay, is non-diversification, or having two many eggs in too few baskets. Modern portfolio theory asserts that capitalism will not pay us for the risk to which we expose ourselves by being too heavily concentrated in one security or a few securities. In other words, the risk associated with having too heavy concentrations in too few risky assets is like walking back and forth across the street a dozen times before we walk into the office in the morning. It is a risk, the exposure to which, capitalism simply will not pay.

ZERO-SUM AND NEGATIVE-SUM GAMES

Non-economic risks may also be looked at as man-made or artificially contrived risks. The risk of unnecessarily walking back and forth across the street is an artificially contrived risk. The risk in a poker game is man-made or artificially contrived and non-economic. Capitalism will not pay us for playing poker.

Poker is also what is known as a "zero-sum" game. A zero-sum game is one in which the total gains of all the winners exactly equals the total losses of all the losers. By definition, there is no net economic benefit to the players collectively (or to society as a whole) in a zero-sum game.

If poker is played in a casino where the house takes something out of each pot, our zero-sum game becomes a "negative-sum game." In a negative-sum game all players, over time, may be expected to lose.

Derivative securities may be classified as negative-sum games. A derivative security represents an artificially contrived risk that rides piggy-back on, or is tied to, some asset that represents a true economic risk.

The most popular derivative security is the call option which depends for its value upon the behavior of some underlying common stock. Player #1 may be willing to purchase a call on a stock under the presumption that the stock is currently undervalued and that it will rise over the next few months. Player #2 may be willing to take the other side of Player #1's bet by going "short" a call (selling to Player #1 a call Player #2 does not own) with the expectation that the stock is overvalued and so both stock and option will drop in price over the next few months. The options exchange obligingly creates a contract for the two players and, at expiration, one player, in theory, has lost exactly what the other player has gained.

In theory, then, our players have created a zero-sum game. In practice, however, they are really playing a negative-sum game. That is because the house does, indeed, take something out of the pot — namely commissions and taxes on the transactions.

THE RELATIVITY OF RISK

In spite of our effort to make a fine distinction between volatility and risk and our effort, shortly, to assign asset categories on the spectrum of uncertainty, it is also useful to acknowledge that risk, in addition to being an attribute of the asset in question, is also a function of the investor for whom the risk is being assessed. What may be a risky asset for one investor may not be a risky asset for another. For an investor with a short investment time horizon, volatility may be construed as risk; and, conversely, given a long investment time horizon, what might have seemed like risk becomes nothing more than volatility.

As an example, let us suppose that Investor #1 and Investor #2 each purchase *ten*-year U.S. Treasury bonds. Investor #1 purchases his bonds with money he has earmarked to build a house in *two* years; Investor #2 purchases his bonds with money he has earmarked for retirement in *ten* years. Let us further suppose that interest rates spike upwards over the next two years. When interest rates go up, bond prices go down. Investor #1, then, loses money on his bonds when he sells them, two years hence, to build his house; Investor #2, however, runs no risk whatever of a money loss because he will hold his bonds until maturity, and he knows they will mature at par. Clearly, the very same asset has been risky for Investor #1 but not risky for Investor #2.

The maturity risk on bonds, of course, is one that is easily controlled. Investor #1 simply need not put into a ten-year bond money he knows he wants to spend in two years; he can purchase a two-year note, instead. For equities, which have no maturities, however, the distinction between risk and volatility, relative to each investor, can be more problematic. Ascertaining whether an investor's assumption of a given degree of uncertainty entails an *unacceptable* level of risk or an *acceptable* level of volatility is the essence of determining the suitability of that investment to the investor's investment time horizon.[4]

Let us now examine the various major asset categories, item-by-item, to try to understand better the extent to which each is an investment and the extent to which each is a gamble and to see why it appears where it does on the revised expected return chart.

CASH

That investment entailing the least uncertainty is cash. If we put cash under our mattress, we always know how much we have (provided it is not stolen or our house does not burn down). We also know exactly what our rate of return will be for as long as it is kept in that location. It will, of course, be zero.

If we put cash in the bank, we always know how much money we have and we can always know when the bank pays its interest but, because the rates paid by banks vary over time, we do have some volatility or uncertainty as to what our future rates of return will be. For accepting this uncertainty, we are paid a modest return.

With our cash in the form of U.S. Treasury bills (U.S. Government securities with maturities of less than one year), in addition to the uncertainty about future rates of interest, we are subject to the possibility of a modest loss (or gain) if we need to sell our bills before they mature. For this higher level of uncertainty, we are paid a slightly higher return.

HIGH QUALITY BONDS

"High quality" bonds are generally defined as those carrying Standard & Poor's ratings of AAA, AA, or A or Moody's ratings of Aaa, Aa, or A. ("Investment Grade" includes, also, bonds rated BBB by S&P or Baa by Moody's.)

Though, with high quality bonds, we are assured of fixed semi-annual payments of interest, we are exposed to variations in the resale price of the bonds, in the event that we should elect to sell them before maturity. If interest rates go up between the time we purchase a bond and the time it matures, and we sell the bond during that interim, we shall probably incur a loss; similarly, if interest rates go down during that period, we may enjoy a gain in the price of the bond (subject to call features).

Changes in the prevailing level of interest rates can dramatically change the resale price of a bond before maturity, and so change significantly the total return on the bond for its owner. Other things (coupon and quality) being equal, the longer the maturity of a bond, the greater the degree of uncertainty in its total return, if not held to maturity.

Given two bonds of the same maturity and quality, the bond with the lower coupon will also be the more volatile. That is because less of the bondholder's return comes in the form of fixed semi-annual coupon payments, and so his total return is more sensitive to changes in interest rates. For this reason, other things (maturity and quality) being equal, zero coupon bonds are more volatile than bonds which pay interest semi-annually.

For accepting this greater uncertainty in the ownership of bonds, therefore, capitalism pays the bondholder more than it does the holder of cash.

COMMON STOCKS

Historically the prices of common stocks have been more volatile than the prices of bonds; and, because so much of their total returns have come from capital appreciation, as opposed to dividend income, the timing of their returns has been even more uncertain than that of bonds.

We define "high-quality" stocks as those carrying Standard & Poor's ratings of A+, A, or A-. As a frame of reference, at any given time, approximately 40% of the stocks in both the Dow-Jones Industrial Average and the Standard & Poor's 500 Index carry these "A" category ratings.

Income stocks have dividend yields that are *above* average while growth stocks have dividend yields that are *below* average.[5] To be classified as a growth stock, we require that a stock have a Value Line "Timeliness" rating of #1 or #2.

For us to classify a stock as "high-quality growth," then, it must have both a Standard & Poor's rating of A+, A, or A- and a Value Line "Timeliness" rating of #1 or #2. To be classified as "aggressive growth," we require that a stock carry a Value Line "Timeliness" rating of #1 or #2, but we waive the S&P hurdle for quality.

On the chart, it will be noticed that "Aggressive Growth Stocks" fall on the border line between "investing" and "gambling." These stocks are decidedly the most volatile within the domain of "investing", and many fall into the domain of "risk" whereby one needs, indeed, to be prepared for the possibility of permanent loss.[6]

Because of their greater volatility, then, common stocks have, historically, delivered higher rates of return than have either cash or bonds.

OBJECTIVITY AND SUBJECTIVITY IN ASSIGNING THE REMAINING ASSET CATEGORIES

The degree of uncertainty (volatility and risk) and the expected return that one assigns to a given category of assets depends, in part, upon how one defines the category and the period of time over which the category's behavior is observed.

In the domain of investing, there is general agreement with respect to the historical degrees of volatility and the hierarchy of expected rates of return experienced with the various asset categories. With respect to the historical behavior of the asset categories in the domain of risk, however, agreement is less universal.

For this chapter, in so far as the writer is aware of historical supporting data, the relative assignments of the several asset categories within the domain of risk is objective; and, to the extent that he draws upon three and one half decades of observing the investment experiences of others, they are subjective.

REAL ESTATE INVESTMENT TRUSTS (REITS)

A real estate investment trust (REIT) provides a good example of a security for which investors commonly sacrifice some expected total return and some degree of safety for the satisfaction of receiving high current income. Studies indicate that REITs have been more volatile and have delivered a lower rate of return than the Standard & Poor's 500. REITs also tend to be highly interest rate sensitive — so much so that, during the credit crunch of the 1970s, great numbers of REITs went bankrupt. On the basis of history, then, the possibility of a permanent loss in the ownership of REITs is relatively high.[7]

JUNK BONDS

Junk bonds are defined as those carrying Standard & Poor's or Moody's ratings that are below investment grade (below BBB or Baa). In explaining its ratings, Standard & Poor's says, "Debt rated [below BBB] is regarded, on balance, as predominantly speculative with respect to capacity to pay interest and repay principal in accordance with the terms of the obligation…While such debt will likely have some quality and protective characteristics, these are outweighed by large uncertainties or major risk exposures to adverse conditions."

Needless to say, junk bonds are risky, in every sense of the word. The consequences of bearing such risk, however, would be far more likely to strike during a severe recession or during a period of unusually high interest rates.

The reason junk bonds have appeal to some investors is that, as with REITs, they provide unusually high current returns. The trade-off for this high current return is a lesser total return over time and the very real risk of a significant loss of principal.[8]

CONVERTIBLE BONDS

Most convertible bonds are junk bonds and so also harbor high risk. Their attractions are a higher current income than on a typical common stock, an appearance of safety by virtue of being a bond, and the potential for appreciation by being convertible into stock. For this "best of both worlds" illusion investors are willing to accept lesser total returns.[9]

SPECULATIVE TURNAROUND STOCKS

The companies that underlie speculative turnaround stocks are similar to the companies that typically issue convertible bonds. They are financially weak. Speculative turnaround stocks do carry the possibility of spectacular gains if their turnarounds are successful (the "lottery" factor). Because most speculative turnaround companies do not get turned around, however, the net return on a basket of such companies tends to be sub par.

EMERGING GROWTH STOCKS

Emerging growth companies are companies, most of which have come to market recently via initial public offerings, and which are still struggling in their infancies. They include the small high-technology stocks of the current era — the Internet and bio-medical companies, many of which are not yet generating profits. Their stock prices are propelled by the public's imagination as to how extraordinarily successful such a company can be, if all goes according to plan.

So glamorous are the prospects in such an industry, however, that many more participants are attracted into it than the industry can accommodate. Though the industry may grow at a phenomenal pace, most participants lose market share at an even faster pace, and so fail to prosper.

Though the excitement of the "lottery" factor is very much in play with the emerging growth stock sector of the stock market, the odds are so heavily stacked against the success of each individual company in it, that most participants in this sector experience sub par returns.

INITIAL PUBLIC OFFERINGS (IPOs)

Initial public offerings (IPOs) typically sell at a premium to their true worth as investments and so deliver sub par returns for three reasons: (1) They tend to be intensively marketed at the time of issuance and so bid up in price above their inherent worth; (2) they carry with them the excitement of enabling the purchaser to get in on the ground floor; and (3) some IPOs have done extraordinarily well in the marketplace (the "lottery" factor). On average, however, IPOs have not done well for most people who have acquired them.[10]

EMERGING MARKETS

Emerging market stocks offer the possibility of above-average gains, if capitalism in the less-developed nations in which they are located blossoms and thrives. As was driven home in 1998, however, the emerging markets are extremely risky and vulnerable. All of the gains accrued in most emerging stock markets over the previous ten years were annihilated in just a few months in 1998.

GOLD AND OTHER PRECIOUS METALS

Gold and other precious metals are commodities, as opposed to productive assets, and, as such, do not generate positive returns, over and above the rate of inflation, when held over long periods of time.

In addition to the entertainment value of trying to time the precious metals cycles, there may even be a prestige or snob factor in the ownership of gold. In any event it has been a very poor investment for most people who have held it.[11]

LIMITED PARTNERSHIPS

It appears that limited partnerships are acquired, in spite of their historically dismal results, in part, because of their heavy promotion by many so-called financial planners who derive extraordinary commissions by selling them. Limited partnerships, too, may carry some degree of snob appeal because their purchase is usually limited to individuals who meet certain minimums of income and/or net worth.

Typically, limited partnerships are highly or totally illiquid. In the past, they have commonly been vehicles designed to exploit loopholes in the Internal Revenue Code. Much of the money that has been lost in such limited partnerships has been the consequence of Congress' subsequently passing legislation that closed the loopholes before the limited partnerships had closed.

HEDGE FUNDS

In its plain vanilla form, a hedge fund uses half its money to buy stocks long and the other half to sell stocks short. By so doing, in theory, it insulates itself from the volatility of the stock market as a whole. If the market goes up, it gains on the long side what it loses on the short side; and, if the market goes down, it gains on the short side what it loses on the long side. If the hedge fund is to make money, however, it must buy stocks that go up *more* (or down less) than the market and/or sell short stocks that go down *more* (or up less) than the market.

Though this is the basic theory of hedging, hedge funds tend to be far more complex, using bonds, derivative securities, and leverage (borrowed money) to implement their strategies.

Unlike mutual funds, hedge funds (which are actually limited partnerships) are not required to disclose their holdings; hence, much of what we know about them is anecdotal. Suffice it to say, however, that 1998 was not a good year for hedge funds. In 1998, the world's largest (and previously most esteemed) hedge fund, Long-Term Capital Management, after just four years in operation under the direction of a Wall Street "dream team" that included former Federal Reserve Board Vice Chairman, David Mullins, and two Nobel Laureates, Robert Merton and Myron Scholes, imploded. Its participants lost over 90% of their investments, and some of its partners were threatened with personal bankruptcy because of money they borrowed personally to invest in the fund. On the basis of his last-minute rescue actions, it also became apparent that the current Fed Chairman, Alan Greenspan, feared that the complete collapse of Long-Term Capital Management might have brought the banking system of the rest of the world down with it.

STOCK OPTIONS

As explained earlier, stock options are zero-sum games in theory and, because of transaction costs, negative-sum games in practice. Stock options, as do all derivative securities, represent artificially-contrived, man-made risks. All participants must be net losers if they play the game long enough.

The purchase of a call is an example of the "lottery" factor at work, while the sale of a call is an example of the "current return" trade-off at work.

COMMODITIES FUTURES

As pointed out under the discussion of gold and other precious metals, commodities are non-productive assets and so generate no economic return. Over the long-term, by holding a commodity, one might expect a return equal to the rate of inflation, less carrying charges, which charges may well exceed the rate of inflation.

Commodities futures contracts, like stock option contracts, are man-made, artificially contrived risks that behave as zero-sum games in theory and negative-sum gains in practice. Futures represent the leveraged ownership of commodities, which magnifies one's interim gains and losses, and so accelerates the timing of the ultimate, long-term, inevitably adverse outcome.

CASINO GAMBLING

Casino gambling represents negative-sum gaming in its purest form.

LOTTERIES

Lotteries, of course, represent the most extreme form of gambling.

MUTUAL FUNDS AND DEFERRED ANNUITIES

Where, one might ask, do mutual funds and variable deferred annuities fit into this picture.

The answer is that they lie on another curve somewhere below the curve we have so far been discussing. This other curve is illustrated by the dotted curve in the accompanying chart. Just where on the horizontal axis of uncertainty any mutual fund or deferred annuity sub-account[12] is located depends upon how it is invested. If it is a money market mutual fund, it will be far to the left; if it is a high-quality bond or stock fund, it will also be to the left of the vertical dashed line that separates investing from gambling; if it is a junk bond, convertible bond, emerging market, or speculative turn-around stock mutual fund, it will fall to the right of the vertical dashed line where the gambling factor begins to prevail.

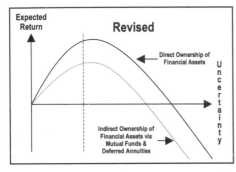

The expected return gap between the solid curve representing investing directly, and the dotted curve representing investing indirectly, varies with both the species of indirect investment (mutual fund or deferred annuity sub-account) and with how that species is invested. The gap is wide, however. For example, for investors indirectly invested in common stocks via mutual funds versus investors directly invested in common stocks, as measured by the Standard & Poor's 500 Stock Index, the gap in 1998 was 19%. That is, the average mutual fund investor earned 19% less in 1998 than did the average investor who owned his common stocks outright; and, over the past twenty years, variable deferred annuities invested in common stocks have underperformed mutual funds invested in common stocks, on average, by 0.70% per year.[13]

CONCLUSION

It is useful to recognize that some assets deliver lower returns than those available on safer investments by virtue of their entertainment value or the lottery factor associated with them; and some assets deliver lower total returns than other safer assets because of the above average current yields available on them. When acquiring such assets, one should recognize that he is trading away *both* some expected return and some safety for the excitement of being a possible big winner or for the immediate satisfaction of a high current return.

For money that is intended to be deployed largely for investment and only minimally, if at all, for entertainment, it is suggested that one confine his assets largely to those to the left of the dashed vertical line on the accompanying chart.

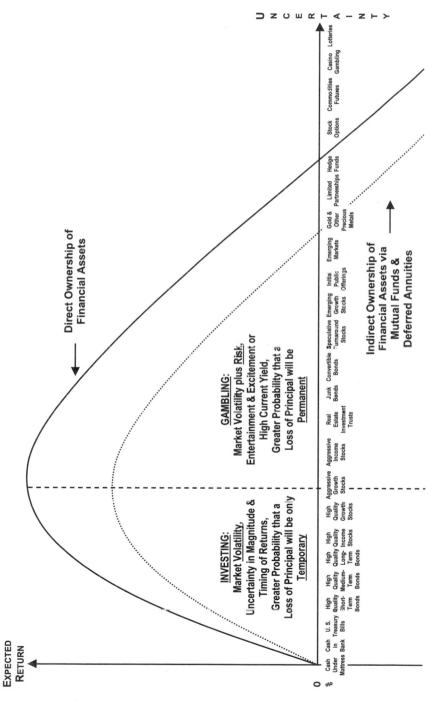

INVESTING VERSUS GAMBLING

EXPECTED RETURN

UNCERTAINTY

Direct Ownership of Financial Assets

Indirect Ownership of Financial Assets via Mutual Funds & Deferred Annuities

INVESTING:
Market Volatility, Uncertainty in Magnitude & Timing of Returns, Greater Probability that a Loss of Principal will be only Temporary

GAMBLING:
Market Volatility plus Risk, Entertainment & Excitement or High Current Yield, Greater Probability that a Loss of Principal will be Permanent

Cash Under Mattress | Cash in Bank | U.S. Treasury Bills | High Quality Short-Term Bonds | High Quality Medium-Term Bonds | High Quality Long-Term Bonds | High Quality Income Stocks | High Quality Growth Stocks | Aggressive Growth Stocks | Aggressive Income Stocks | Real Estate Investment Trusts | Junk Bonds | Convertible Bonds | Speculative Turnaround Stocks | Emerging Growth Stocks | Initial Public Offerings | Emerging Markets | Gold & Other Precious Metals | Limited Partnerships | Hedge Funds | Stock Options | Commodities Futures | Casino Gambling | Lotteries

Chapter 1 Footnotes:

[1] For purposes of this chapter, "safety" refers to safety of "principal," as opposed to safety of "purchasing power."

[2] For Assets A and B, assume that the average *absolute* rates of return over some period have been 8% and 4% per year respectively; the *relative* return on A, then, would have been *twice* that on B; the *hierarchical* return on A, however, would have been simply *greater* than that on B, with neither how much greater, nor the ratio of their magnitudes, being specified.

[3] Security analysts use the term "duration" to describe and, in the case of bonds, to measure, the degree of uncertainty in the timing of the return on an investment. For example, all other things being equal, a low-coupon or zero coupon bond has a longer "duration" than a high coupon bond. Longer maturities also produce longer durations. All other things being equal, a high dividend paying stock would have a shorter duration than a low dividend paying stock.

[4] Other important suitability considerations include the investor's personal *tolerance* for risk and volatility and his income tax and estate tax circumstances.

[5] The category of high quality *income* stocks is almost an oxymoron because so few such companies exist. A common stock usually has a yield that is *above* average *because* its quality is *below* average.

[6] One of the more common categorizations of common stocks is by capitalization (i.e., large cap, medium cap, small cap, and microcap). It is this writer's conviction, however, that such distinctions are not useful in the common stock selection process, and so these categories are not used here. For more on the subject of "large cap" versus "small cap" investing, please see that subject on our web site.

[7] For more on REITs, please see that subject on our web site.

[8] For more on junk bond ratings, please see that subject on our web site.

[9] For more on convertible bonds, please see that subject on our web site.

[10] For more on IPOs, please see that subject on our web site.

[11] For more on gold and precious metals, please see that subject on our web site.

[12] Technically, the investments offered by variable deferred annuities are "sub-accounts." Except for the fact that their expense ratios are usually higher, for all practical purposes, deferred annuity sub-accounts behave exactly like, and are usually called, mutual funds.

[13] In 1998 the S&P 500 delivered a total return of 28.34% while the Wiesenberger composite of all equity mutual funds showed a total return of 9.74%. Over the 20 years ending with 1998, the Wiesenberger equity mutual fund composite returned an average of 15.28% per year while the Wiesenberger all equity variable annuity composite returned an average of 14.58% per year.

2

EFFICIENCY AND THE CONTROL OF RISK: THE ESSENCE OF SUCCESSFUL PORTFOLIO MANAGEMENT

The purpose of this chapter is not to pontificate on how one should invest his money. Our clients already know that we have few inhibitions expounding on that score. The intent here is to suggest the appropriate subjects of scrutiny for those interested in how their money is managed, whether they manage it themselves or have somebody else manage it for them.

Contents

AREAS OF FOCUS

There appear to be three major areas upon which one might focus in the management of an investment portfolio: (1) The nature and degree of risk and volatility to which the portfolio is exposed; (2) the monetary efficiency with which the portfolio functions; and (3) the rate of return that the portfolio generates.

It is my personal impression, in observing the actions and comments of others over the years, and especially so in the years of the great bull market that has persisted with little interruption since August of 1982, that more and more investors focus, first and predominantly, upon performance and rates of return, with the issues of risk and efficiency less well understood and so largely neglected.

It is my belief that, if one wishes truly to maximize the probability of long-term investment success which, in the future, may entail coping with bear markets as well as bull markets, recessions as well as recoveries, credit crunches as well as periods of declining interest rates, and conceivably even deflation or depression, as well as inflation, disinflation, and economic boom, the prioritizing of, and emphasis on, the three above-mentioned considerations should be as follows:

1. A portfolio's exposure to risk should be, overwhelmingly, the *primary* consideration.

2. Though secondary, the matter of efficiency should be given *intense* consideration.

3. The issue of performance and rates of return should be a *non-*consideration.

PERFORMANCE AND RATES OF RETURN

We shall have more to say about performance and rates of return farther on. At this point, however, let us explain briefly why this subject is relegated to such a low position on the above totem pole. The answer is that, after we have made the decisions about the exposure of our portfolio to risk and volatility and have attempted to optimize the efficiency with which our portfolio functions, we no longer have any control over its performance and rate of return.

Safety and return are correlated inversely and rigidly, as are the two ends of a teeter board. To try to push one end up with the expectation that the other end will not go down is futile.

Furthermore, it seems pretty safe to say that, though investors vary widely with respect to their individual tolerances for risk and volatility, they all share the common goal of wanting to *maximize* the after-tax rates of return on their portfolios.

DEFINITIONS OF "LOSS," "RISK," AND "VOLATILITY"

There are two kinds of financial loss. We can lose our principal and/or we can lose our purchasing power. We lose our principal when we buy a stock at $50 per share and sell it at $25 per share; and we lose purchasing power when we hold bonds for a quarter of a century, during which inflation averages 3%, and so are able to purchase only half the goods and services with the bonds' principal at the end of the period as we could have at the beginning.

Let us define "risk" as the "*possibility* of a loss that is *permanent*" and "volatility" as the "*probability* that losses will be only *temporary*."

Let us further recognize a gray area between risk and volatility. What, for a long investment time horizon portfolio, may be simple volatility, for a shorter time horizon, may be bona fide risk. While a twenty-year U.S. Government bond presumably poses no risk of money loss for the investor who puts it away for twenty years, it poses the possibility of a considerable money loss for one who might choose to sell it in five or ten years.[1]

HOW TO CONTROL RISK AND VOLATILITY

There are four important ways in which we can control the nature and magnitude of the risk and volatility to which a portfolio is exposed:

[1] asset allocation

[2] security diversification

[3] quality discrimination

[4] market risk modification

ASSET ALLOCATION

Asset allocation is the deployment of one's financial resources among various asset categories. In an earlier era, asset allocation typically referred to the disposition of a portfolio among the three major asset classes — cash, bonds, and common stocks. In more recent times, the asset allocation decision has come to include sub-categories of these three major asset classes, as well as new categories outside the traditional three. Within the universe of common stocks, for example, one might select among growth, income, value, and cyclical stocks, or among large-cap, mid-cap, small-cap, and micro-cap stocks. Other asset categories now commonly used in the asset allocation process include convertible bonds, real estate investment trusts, venture capital, gold, foreign securities, limited partnerships, options, and commodities futures. In fact, the number of financial assets to which allocations might be made is limited only by the imagination of the asset allocator.

Needless to say, the simplest way to minimize the exposure of a portfolio to volatility and the risk of a money loss is to keep it invested in cash — bank CDs, money market funds, or U.S. Treasury bills. Unfortunately, such a strategy also maximizes the portfolio's exposure to the risk of a purchasing power loss and minimizes its expected return. In search of higher returns, then, investors venture out to bonds, common stocks, and other more volatile and riskier assets.

It is important to recognize that arriving at an optimum asset allocation is more a personal than a financial decision. Whether one should be 100% in cash, 100% in common stocks, or somewhere in between depends upon one's personal tolerance for volatility and risk. There is no "one-size-fits-all" financially correct asset allocation, nor is there any mathematical formula for arriving at an appropriate asset allocation for any individual investor.

The asset allocation decision is often compared to one of choosing between "eating" well and "sleeping" well. While there is, hopefully for everyone, some choice that will permit both, the analogy does illustrate how truly subjective the asset allocation decision is.

If we are confused by the great proliferation of options in the asset allocation process, it is suggested that a simple return to basics will go far toward resolving the issue. If we think in terms of just cash, bonds, and common stocks, and allocate accordingly, most of the risk control available in the asset allocation decision will have been achieved.[2]

DIVERSIFICATION

Assuming that we are going to venture beyond cash, we, then, become interested in the second way of controlling volatility and risk — diversification.

Diversification refers to the ownership of securities within the same asset category but of different issuers. In the case of corporate bonds and common stocks, diversification implies not having a heavy concentration in the security of any one company or even in the securities of companies in any one industry.

When taking initial positions in securities, diversification is not a difficult objective to pursue. One merely makes sure his commitment to each new acquisition is modest in size. Nor is it difficult to maintain good diversification in a tax-sheltered account. If one has the good fortune to own a common stock that appreciates so much that his portfolio becomes heavily concentrated in it, the size of the position can be pruned without any tax consequence. In a taxable account, however, the sale of a highly appreciated common stock for the purpose of diversifying can be a less pleasant experience.

Even in the best of times, what appeared to be a good common stock can go sour. Diversification, then, is a strategy for bull markets as well as bear markets. Good diversification is achieved to the extent that an isolated precipitous decline in the price of an individual security in a portfolio would not be an overly emotional experience.

As a rule-of-thumb, initial stock positions probably ought not exceed 5%, and initial industry positions probably ought not exceed 10%, of the value of a portfolio; and, when a single issue grows to 10%, or an industry position grows to 20%, of the entire value of a portfolio, the situation might become worrisome.[3]

QUALITY DISCRIMINATION

It is in the area of quality discrimination that investors seem to be most at sea in controlling the risk to which they expose their portfolios. It is my personal impression that great numbers of investors give little consideration to the quality of the securities they own and, of those concerned with quality, many are uncertain about how to measure it.

One of the ironies of the issue of quality is that common stock investors usually give even less consideration to this factor than do bond investors. This is so, in spite of the fact that the common stock of a given company is always riskier than even the lowest quality bond of that same company. In other words, though a focus on quality would seem to be of critical importance in either instance, it would seem to be of even greater importance to a common stock investor than to a bond investor.

DETERMINING THE QUALITY OF A COMMON STOCK OR BOND

There is more than one way to measure the quality of a security. We usually do it with Standard & Poor's ratings. S&P common stock ratings are based upon the growth and stability of a company's earnings and dividends over the previous ten years. In explaining the rationale of its approach, S&P says the following:

> The investment process involves assessment of various factors — such as products and industry position, corporate resources and financial policy — with results that make some common stocks more highly esteemed than others. In this assessment, Standard & Poor's believes that earnings and dividend performance is the end result of the interplay of these factors and that, over the long run, the record of this performance has a considerable bearing on relative quality.

Capital structure, for example, is indirectly reflected in these ratings in that a highly leveraged balance sheet would generate a more volatile earnings record and so a lower S&P rating.

A Value Line "Financial Strength" rating might be used as a measure of quality except that its emphasis is largely on the balance sheet, and so it gives less recognition to the nature of the business in which the company operates. Because of the stability of its industry, for example, a pharmaceutical company should be able to tolerate comfortably more debt in its capital structure than a cyclical automobile company or a company in the rapidly evolving computer industry.[4]

A Value Line "Safety" rating might also be used as a measure of quality. This rating is a combination of a company's "Financial Strength" rating and the relative *volatility* of its stock over some period of time. If, however, we define "quality" as a measure of the reliability of the underlying company, if we reserve the concept of "market risk" (which we shall discuss shortly) for issues dealing with the pricing of a common stock relative to these fundamentals, and if we distinguish between "risk" and "volatility," the Value Line "Safety" rating seems like a hybrid that is both redundant and superfluous.

MEASURING THE QUALITY OF A PORTFOLIO

Measuring the quality of a whole portfolio of securities using Standard & Poor's quality ratings is a bit more complex than looking up the rating on an individual issue. It is, however, a technique easily available to anybody who wants to spend a little time at it; and doing so could be as important to one's financial well being as taking one's blood pressure could be to his physical well being.

If one is measuring the quality of a bond portfolio, he needs a Standard & Poor's Bond Guide; and, if he is measuring the quality of a common stock portfolio, he needs a Standard & Poor's Stock Guide. Most libraries carry these publications, and one's broker will usually be happy to send one to a client. The guides are published monthly but, for our purposes here, a several-month-old copy is nearly as good as an up-to-date one. The S&P rating on a specific bond or common stock does not change very often.

Most widely held bonds and stocks carry S&P quality ratings. High quality bonds carry ratings of AAA, AA, or A and high-quality stocks carry ratings of A+, A, or A-. Medium quality bonds carry the rating BBB, and medium quality stocks carry the rating B+. Bonds with ratings lower than BBB are called "junk" (or, euphemistically, "high-yield") bonds; and, similarly, we call stocks rated lower than B+ "junk" stocks.

A "Portfolio Quality Index" (PQI) for a bond or stock portfolio can be calculated as follows:

	CURRENT $ VALUE OF HOLDING		
Stock or Bond	Stocks: S&P= A+, A, or A- Bonds: S&P= AAA, AA, or A	Stocks: S&P= B+ Bonds: S&P= BBB	All Other Issues
Issue #1	$	$	$
Issue #2	$	$	$
Issue #3	$	$	$
etc.	etc.	etc.	etc.
Total Value	$X	$Y	$Z

$$\text{Portfolio Quality Index (PQI)} = \frac{\$X + \dfrac{\$Y}{2}}{\$X + \$Y + \$Z}$$

The PQI may then be interpreted as follows:

PQI	CLASSIFICATION
80% to 100%	Highest
60% to 80%	Above Average
40% to 60%	Average[5]
20% to 40%	Below Average
0% to 20%	Lowest

MEASURING THE QUALITY OF A MUTUAL FUND

One of the reasons that the issue of portfolio quality tends to be less visible than it might be is that so many people today own their securities via the intermediary of a mutual fund or a variable annuity sub-account. While the shareholder may know the name of his mutual fund, he is unlikely to be familiar with the names of the companies held by the fund on his behalf. There is, further, the dangerous assumption made by some that mutual funds are all about the same.

The quality of the underlying holdings in a mutual fund is a very important issue. There are over 10,000 mutual funds in existence today, which is over five times as many stocks as there are on the New York Stock Exchange, and the quality of their portfolios ranges from the sublime to the ridiculous. Furthermore, being judged largely upon performance alone, mutual funds have tended to hold increasingly aggressive, lower quality portfolios in recent years.

One way of measuring the quality of a mutual fund portfolio is to get a copy of the portfolio and use the technique described above. Because so many mutual funds hold well over one-hundred different issues, however, this may not be an easy task.

A good alternative is to use a page on the fund from the Morningstar or CDA/Wiesenberger service which will show the fund's top twenty-five or so holdings.[6] The presumption that might be made is that the rest of the fund's portfolio is of the same quality character as its largest holdings.[7]

1998 — AN EXAMPLE OF A PAYBACK FOR QUALITY

Incorporating high-quality in a common stock portfolio is comparable to buying fire insurance on our house. In particular, we do not need it unless we have a fire. Similarly, we really have not needed portfolio insurance during most of the current great bull market which got underway in August of 1982.

1998, however, was instructive. It was the year that the economies and currencies of the Far East went into free fall, and those of Latin America followed suit. Investors around the world became increasingly concerned about the possibility of global depression, deflation, and even an international monetary collapse. The result was what is known as a "flight to safety" or a "flight to quality." Money invested in these so-called "emerging" markets left those markets and came to the United States as a safer haven, causing the emerging markets to go down and the U.S. markets to be buoyed up. Similarly, money invested in low-quality U.S. securities was redeployed into issues of higher-quality, causing the latter to outperform the former. Just how one might have protected himself from the ensuing stock market carnage by maintaining a portfolio with a respectable "Portfolio Quality Index" is illustrated in the following table:

IMPACT OF THE 1998 FLIGHT TO QUALITY ON MUTUAL FUND PORTFOLIOS OF VARYING QUALITY

Market Sector	Average PQI 12/31/97 to 9/11/98	% Total Return
Latin America Funds	0%	-52.24%
Diversified Emerging Market Funds	0%	-39.24%
U.S. Small Cap Funds	18%	-18.10%
U.S. Mid-Cap Funds	25%	-8.50%
U.S. Large Cap Funds	77%	+1.92%

The above computations are derived from data found in the Standard & Poor's and Morningstar Mutual Fund services.

MARKET RISK MODIFICATION

Market risk refers to the vulnerability of a security uniquely attributable to the level of its price. Market risk may manifest itself in the collapse of a security's price, either because of a change in the investment community's perception of that particular company or because of a change in the community's perception of the entire industry or other category of which that particular security is a member.

MODIFYING MARKET RISK IN A BOND PORTFOLIO

For a high-quality bond or a high-quality bond portfolio, market risk is almost synonymous with "interest rate" risk. Falling interest rates tend to push the prices of bonds up, while rising rates tend to push them down.

We can modify our market risk in a bond portfolio by modifying the average maturity of the bonds in the portfolio. If we lengthen the average maturity of the portfolio, we increase our exposure to market risk; and, if we shorten the average maturity, we lessen our exposure to market risk.

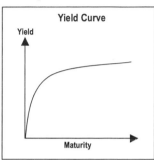

One common tool for trying to control market risk in a bond portfolio is the "yield curve." The yield curve is a plot of bond maturities on the horizontal axis and bond yields on the vertical axis, as seen in the chart to the right. The traditional yield curve rises sharply in the early years and more gradually in the later years. It is often argued that an optimum maturity for buying bonds is at the break in the yield curve, or where the curve turns most sharply from steep to relatively flat.[8] It is felt that, at this maturity, one has reached a point of diminishing returns, in that exposing oneself to the risk of still longer maturities produces too little incremental return.[9]

In recent years, the break in the yield curve has commonly occurred at about three- to five-year maturities. At such times, though owning longer maturities would have exacerbated market risk, there would appear to have been little in the way of additional return available for doing so.

MODIFYING MARKET RISK IN A COMMON STOCK PORTFOLIO

In the case of common stocks, we can control market risk by modifying the price-earnings ratios to which we allow our portfolio to be exposed.[10] A useful tool for this purpose is what is known as the "relative price-earnings ratio" which ratio is published by the Value Line service for the companies it covers, and can be easily calculated, in any event.[11] If a common stock sells at a relative price-earnings ratio of 1.50, for example, we might conclude that it harbors a market risk that is 50% greater than that of the average common stock.[12]

As a rule-of-thumb, it might be prudent to consider pruning large positions in stocks with relative price earnings ratios in excess of 2.00.[13]

Probably the best example of the potential consequences of exposing a common stock portfolio to excess market risk is the collapse of the so-called "nifty fifty" in the early 1970s. The nifty fifty was a group of large capitalization growth stocks which, at their peak, had price-earnings ratios that averaged 42-to-1 and relative price-earnings ratios that averaged 2.2-to-1. During the bear market that followed, while the market as a whole (as measured by the Standard & Poor's 500) declined by 48%, the nifty-fifty, collectively, declined 62%, with some stocks in the group declining over 90%.[14]

EFFICIENCY IN THE MANAGEMENT OF A PORTFOLIO

With the stock market's having been so extravagantly rewarding to almost everybody who has participated in it over the past seventeen years, there does not seem to have been a great deal of emphasis by investors placed upon efficiency. If one earned the 10% produced by the average equity mutual fund in 1998, he may have been less concerned over the fact that the stock market, as measured by the Standard & Poor's 500 Stock Index, returned 29%, and so he should have been able to earn 29% simply by selecting stocks at random from the index and never bothering to manage his portfolio thereafter. After all, even after the 19% shortfall is subtracted from the 29% return, the investor still nets 10% — hardly catastrophic.

If, however, one is willing to recognize that stock market returns, historically, have averaged 11% per year, not 29% per year, and that bond returns have averaged less than half what the stock market has averaged, he will soon realize that the efficiency with which stocks and bonds are owned can be a very important factor over the long term.

Let me provide an example of the ultimate in inefficient portfolio management. An individual recently told me of an investment firm meeting he had attended, sponsored by a competitor of ours. He said that the firm was advising people to employ it to help them find a service which, in turn, would help select and monitor a manager who would manage a portfolio of mutual funds for them. The individual wondered what ever was happening at that firm to the old fashioned broker who, himself, used to help clients assemble and manage investment portfolios.

Contemplate the absurdity of what this individual had observed. People were being asked to pay a brokerage firm to engage a service to select a manager who would second guess mutual fund managers who, in turn, are trying to second guess corporate managers. Paying for five levels of management service can, indeed, detract considerably from the efficiency of investing.

The essence of efficiency in the management of one's investments is *not* paying for services that add negligible value to the investment process. The greatest irony of all, however, is that so many services for which investors pay dearly actually impact negatively upon their returns. They are not only no better off for utilizing the services, they are worse off.

SOURCES OF INVESTMENT INEFFICIENCY

The most conspicuous sources of investment inefficiencies are mutual funds, variable annuities, and fee-based managed accounts which, in turn, invest in investment products rather than hold the underlying assets.

To understand how one measures inefficiencies in investing, one must first understand the concept of a legitimate market benchmark. A market benchmark is typically a market index which is made up of a representative cross-section of securities of a particular type. For common stocks, the most commonly used benchmark is the Standard & Poor's 500.

When comparing the performance of a portfolio of securities against the Standard & Poor's 500, it should be realized that this index represents large capitalization stocks which, in turn, means that, on average, it consists of higher quality stocks than most other stock market indices.

It should next be realized that, because an index is not actively managed, the performance of a broadly diversified portfolio of stocks, randomly selected from those in the index and never managed thereafter, should approximate the performance of the index. Though such a portfolio is not apt to track the index precisely, it should track the index quite closely; and, furthermore, the likelihood of such a portfolio's performing *better* than the index is just as great as its performing *worse*.

If, over a reasonable period of time, a common stock portfolio, made up of stocks of no higher quality than those in the Standard & Poor's 500, underperforms that index, the inescapable conclusion must be that it is an inefficient investment vehicle. Furthermore, the measure of its inefficiency is no less than the amount by which it underperforms that index.

Nor is it useful, in such an instance, to show how a portfolio may have outperformed a lower quality index such as the Standard & Poor's MidCap or SmallCap index or the Russell 2000. If a portfolio of lower quality securities performs less well than the S&P 500, then, in addition to being less efficient than a portfolio randomly selected from the S&P 500 and unmanaged, it is also more risky. There is no point in taking on *added* risk to reap a *lower* return.

MEASURING THE MAGNITUDE OF INEFFICIENCY

Mutual funds and variable annuities operate in fish bowls, and so the various financial services are able to measure their track records, individually and collectively, with precision.

The following table shows the performance of the average bond mutual fund, relative to the Lehman Brothers Long-Term U.S. Government bond index, and the performance of the average stock mutual fund, relative to the Standard & Poor's 500 Stock Index, over various periods ending December 31, 1998. It also shows the incremental income experienced by the investor invested in the same asset class directly, as opposed to indirectly via mutual funds:

AVERAGE ANNUAL TOTAL RETURN FOR PERIODS ENDING DECEMBER 31, 1998

CATEGORY	1 YEAR	3 YEARS	5 YEARS	10 YEARS	15 YEARS	20 YEARS
U.S. Government Bonds	12.66%	8.75%	9.21%	11.46%	12.56%	11.15%
Bond Mutual Funds	5.12%	5.87%	5.49%	7.55%	8.62%	8.42%
Efficiency Shortfall	7.54%	2.88%	3.72%	3.91%	3.94%	2.73%
Return on Direct Investments vs. Mutual Funds	+147%	+49%	+68%	+52%	+46%	+32%
Common Stocks	28.57%	28.23%	24.06%	19.21%	17.90%	17.75%
Stock Mutual Funds	9.74%	14.69%	13.03%	13.79%	13.34%	15.28%
Efficiency Shortfall	18.83%	13.54%	11.03%	5.42%	4.56%	2.47%
Return on Direct Investments vs. Mutual Funds	+193%	+92%	+85%	+39%	+34%	+16%

Source: CDA/Wiesenberger. Proxy for bond funds = "All Fixed Income" and proxy for stock funds = "All Equity."

As can be seen, over the past twenty years, while an unmanaged list of long-term U.S. Government bonds returned an average of 11.15% per year, the average "professionally" managed bond mutual fund returned only 8.42% per year — an average shortfall of 2.73% per year. Put another way, by owning U.S. Government bonds outright, one earned 32% more than by owning a typical bond mutual fund. Particularly astounding is the nearly tripling of the average annual shortfall from the 20-year average of 2.73% to 7.54% in 1998. (For variable annuities invested in bond funds, the average shortfall over the 20-year period was 4.13% per year, providing the direct investor with a 59% advantage over the variable annuity investor.)

In the case of common stocks, though the mutual fund efficiency short-fall has averaged 2.47% (3.17% for variable annuities) per year over the past twenty years, it has also been growing larger in the more recent periods. In 1998, the efficiency shortfall for the average equity mutual fund was a staggering 18.83% — over seven times the average of the previous twenty years. By owning his stocks outright in 1998, an investor could have earned nearly three times as much on his investments as by owning the average equity mutual fund. The inefficiencies inherent in mutual funds is explained largely by "market impact costs" — the sacrifices in transaction prices institutions must accept in order to buy and sell the large blocks of stocks in which they must deal.[15]

The magnitude of inefficiency in a fee-based managed account depends largely upon the size of the management fee being paid, but also depends upon the magnitude of market impact costs if the management company pools its trades and executes them in large blocks. To the degree that bonds and cash, as opposed to common stocks, are held in a fee-based managed account, the portfolio is apt to be less efficient. That is because the fees charged will probably consume a greater proportion of the total return generated by the bonds and cash over time.

ILLUSTRATIONS OF THE IMPORTANCE OF EFFICIENCY

To see how critical efficiency in our mode of investing can be, let us examine the differences in the results of two investors over various periods of time from one to twenty years. We assume that one investor has invested in common stocks directly while the other has invested in common stocks via mutual funds. Using the data from the preceding table we construct a second table as follows:

TOTAL RETURNS BY INVESTING IN COMMON STOCKS DIRECTLY VS. VIA A MUTUAL FUND OVER VARIOUS PERIODS OF TIME

(Assuming an Initial Investment of $10,000
with Dividends Reinvested in a Tax-Deferred or Tax-Exempt Account)

Period to 12/31/98	1 YEAR		3 YEARS		5 YEARS	
Average T/R of S&P 500	28.57% per year		28.23% per year		24.06% per year	
Mode of Investing	Direct	via M/Fs	Direct	via M/Fs	Direct	via M/Fs
% Shortfall	0.00%	18.83%	0.00%	13.54%	0.00%	11.03%
Net Rate of Return	28.57%	9.74%	28.23%	14.69%	24.06%	13.03%
Value at End of Period	$12,857	$10,974	$21,085	$15,086	$29.387	$18,449
Total Return*	$2,857	$974	$11,085	$5,086	$19,387	$8,449
T/R via Direct Investing Greater than M/F Investing by	193%		118%		129%	
Period to 12/31/98	10 YEARS		15 YEARS		20 YEARS	
Average T/R of S&P 500	19.21% per year		17.90% per year		17.75% per year	
Mode of Investing	Direct	via M/Fs	Direct	via M/Fs	Direct	via M/Fs
% Shortfall	0.00%	5.42%	0.00%	4.56%	0.00%	2.47%
Net Rate of Return	19.21%	13.79%	17.90%	13.34%	17.75%	15.28%
Value at End of Period	$57,960	$33,395	$118,224	$65,426	$262,554	$171,882
Total Return*	$47,960	$23,359	$108,224	$55,426	$252,554	$161,882
T/R via Direct Investing Greater than M/F Investing by	105%		95%		56%	

*Total Return= Value at end of period less initial investment of $10,000.

What is emphasized in this table that is not brought home in the preceding table is the effect of compounding over time. Over the past ten years, for example, merely by avoiding the 5.42% average annual shortfall experienced by the mutual fund investor, the direct investor more than doubled the return on his money.

Efficiency in the management of an investment portfolio clearly can be just as important as the asset allocation decision. An investor may easily negate all the incremental return he expects from owning stocks instead of bonds, or bonds instead of cash, by having his securities held by an inefficient intermediary.

BACK, AGAIN, TO PERFORMANCE AND RATES OF RETURN

As indicated earlier, once an investor has arrived at an allocation of his financial assets to the investment categories with which he is comfortable, after he has established some diversification guidelines, after he has defined the parameters of quality that he requires of his individual investments, after he has put limits on the market risk to which he wants his portfolio exposed, and after he has determined the vehicle by which he will acquire and hold his investments, there is not much room left to influence performance and rates of return.

Admittedly, fine tuning and maintaining the character of a portfolio might consist of: (1) selling a stock that is no longer growing in a growth portfolio and replacing it with one that is; (2) pruning the position in a highly-appreciated stock; (3) replacing a stock or bond that is no longer high-quality in a high-quality portfolio; or (4) lightening or eliminating the position in a stock with an abnormally high price-earnings ratio.

Efficacy in making such decisions, however, is better measured directly by these same criteria than by examining the results achieved after the fact. Inferring how well a portfolio is *managed* by comparing its rate of return with some benchmark is like judging the condition of an airplane by whether we arrive at our destination early, on time, late, or not at all. It is far more comforting to know that somebody has checked out the condition of the craft *before* it takes off, rather than deducing what its condition must have been, after it is on the ground again. Nor should we penalize the pilot if our flight is delayed because he chose to make an extra safety check before take-off.[16]

PAST PERFORMANCE MEASUREMENTS OF MONEY MANAGERS

Fee-based money managers, as do mutual funds, typically market their wares on the basis of the rates of return they demonstrate having achieved for their clients in the past. Because of past abuses in calculating and presenting such data, much effort has been going into the development of uniform "performance presentation standards," whereby managers are all being expected to use the same techniques for measuring and presenting their past performance. To conform to these evolving and increasingly complex standards, money managers are being required to expend considerable time, energy, and money in categorizing their portfolios into composites, adjusting for cash flows in and out of each portfolio, and measuring with precision the total returns generated from one period to the next. The utility of such measurements, however, is questionable for three reasons:

[1] Countless studies, over the past four decades, have demonstrated the validity of the "efficient market hypothesis," which asserts essentially that an investor cannot outperform the market sector in which he invests with a probability greater than that of random chance. Furthermore, when measured in terms of rates of return, there is no positive correlation between the past performance of a money manager and his future performance. Performance measurement, then, is the measurement of "luck," not "skill."[17]

[2] As performance measurement is increasingly refined, it becomes more costly to provide. Such costs must ultimately be borne by the money manager's clients, and so these clients' portfolios become burdened with still greater inefficiency.

[3] Investors utilizing such information, not only derive no benefit from it and pay a price for receiving it, but may be misled into making inappropriate money manager selections by using it.

HOW WE CAN, AND CANNOT, ENHANCE PORTFOLIO RETURN

We can enhance the return on our portfolio by changing our asset allocation and so exposing our portfolio to greater volatility. We *may* be able to enhance its return by exposing it to greater risk. If we win, we enjoy a greater return; if we lose, we experience a lesser return. We may also be able to enhance our return by improving the efficiency with which our portfolio is managed.

We cannot enhance our return by moving back and forth among cash, bonds, and stocks; by moving back and forth between the U.S. stock market and foreign stock markets; by rotating among investment categories; or by trying to exploit mispriced securities in the marketplace. Nor can we enhance our return by employing a money manager to try to do these things for us.

Though, intuitively, we may think it should be possible for somebody to perform these several feats successfully, empirically, we know it is not. The reason we know is because nobody has yet been identified who can perform them with a consistency greater than that of random chance.

CONCLUSION

Learning about investing is as much learning about human limitations and what it is *not* within our power to do, as it is learning about opportunities and what it *is* within our power to do.

If we will focus upon the risks to which we subject our portfolio and the efficiency with which it functions, and leave to fate the rates of return that we are dealt, we shall have done all we can do. Over time, we will do neither better nor worse than others with the same portfolio profile. With the conviction that we have done the best that could humanly be done, we should then be satisfied.

Chapter 2 Footnotes:

[1] The resale price of a bond moves inversely with interest rates and, the longer until the bond matures, the wider the price fluctuations can be.

[2] To make the asset allocation decision still easier, and probably more efficient, it is suggested that one even cast out consideration of bonds. By allocating between just cash and common stocks, historically, one has been able to achieve greater safety, less volatility, and higher returns than by including bonds in a portfolio. Please see the article, "A 'Barbell' Approach to Asset Allocation," on our web site.

[3] For more information on "How Many Stocks to Buy," please see the article by that title on our web site.

[4] Many of the common stocks in a category we call "aggressive growth" do not have long enough histories to have earned S&P ratings. In these cases we defer to the Value Line "Financial Strength" ratings for purposes of quality discrimination.

[5] The PQIs of the Dow-Jones Industrial Average, the Standard & Poor's 500, and the typical index mutual fund, tend to gravitate around 50%.

[6] In the case of many bond portfolios Morningstar conveniently calculates for us the "average credit quality" of the entire portfolio.

[7] Actually, this may be a rather generous assumption. That is because mutual funds tend to have their larger holdings in larger capitalization companies which, in turn, tend to be higher quality companies than are smaller capitalization companies. Looking at just the top holdings of a mutual fund, then, is apt to bias its PQI upward.

[8] Mathematicians would refer to this "break" in the yield curve as a "point of inflexion."

[9] Value Line, in its "Selections & Opinions," publishes weekly a U.S. Treasury yield curve to which one might refer.

[10] Besides the price-earnings ratio, other yardsticks frequently used to measure market risk include the price-to-sales ratio, the price-to-cash flow ratio, and the price-to-book ratio.

[11] To calculate a company's relative price-earnings ratio, divide its price-earnings ratio by the price-earnings ratio of the market as a whole.

[12] For more information on price-earnings ratios, relative price-earnings ratios, and a more esoteric concept we call the "relative relative" price-earnings ratio, please see our paper, "High Price-Earnings Ratios and the Control of Risk," on our web site.

[13] Alternatively, one might use a "relative relative" price-earnings ratio of 1.50 as a hurdle rate. Please see the preceding footnote.

[14] For more on the "nifty fifty," please see our paper, "High Price Earnings Ratios and the Control of Risk," on our web site.

[15] For a further explanation of market impact costs and other mutual fund inefficiencies, please see our paper, "Mutual Fund Efficiency and Performance," on our web site.

[16] Alternative analogy: We should not regret having owned a high quality security or a high quality portfolio during a period when low quality does better than high quality anymore than we should regret having spent money on fire insurance on our house during a period when our house did not burn down.

[17] For more on the "efficient market hypothesis," please see our paper, "The Mother of All Hedge Funds and the Efficient Market Hypothesis," on our web site.

3

HIGH-PRICE EARNINGS RATIOS AND THE CONTROL OF RISK

Contents

Let us begin with an overview of the nature of risk in the ownership of common stocks:

THE DETERMINANTS OF RISK

The price of a common stock may be said to be determined by three factors:

[A] The perceived viability of the underlying company and the perceived *reliability* of some level of its future profits: Efforts are made to isolate and measure this component of risk, as with the Standard & Poor's common stock ratings.

[B] The perceived *potential for growth* in the profits of the underlying company: The Value Line "timeliness" ratings are a popular way of trying to get a handle on this dimension.

[C] The rates of interest (or expected rates of interest) at which the above levels of profitability are *capitalized, discounted,* or "evaluated" in the financial marketplace: If, for example, bank certificates of deposit are paying 10%, whatever profitability figures are arrived for a common stock in A and B, above will be of less value than if CDs were paying only 5%.

THE TYPES OF RISK

The element of risk in a common stock is typically broken down into two parts:

[1] The first is *systematic* or *market* risk which describes the risk inherent in the stock market as a whole. Any and all of the foregoing risk factors, A, B, and C, can influence the degree of systematic risk investors perceive in the stock market. If the investing public anticipates turbulent economic times, declining corporate profits, and rising interest rates, the stock market will surely decline and bring nearly all common stocks down with it.

If, on the other hand, investors anticipate a prosperous economy, rising corporate profits, and declining interest rates, the stock market is more apt to rise and, as does a rising tide, raise all ships with it.

[2] The second type of risk is called *unsystematic* or *idiosyncratic* risk. It describes the risk inherent in a particular common stock, over and above the risk in the market as a whole.

Idiosyncratic risk is also a function of the above risk factors, A, B, and C. If a company's anticipated rate of growth is downgraded by the public, the price of its common stock will take a hit; and, if a company's very viability is believed to be in jeopardy, the price of its common stock will suffer even more. Depending upon their lines of business, too, some companies, more than others, are impacted by changes in interest rates.

THE PHILOSOPHY OF COMMON STOCK INVESTING

At least one theory of investing (my own included) accepts market risk as inevitable and unavoidable (and so market timing futile). Market risk is perceived to be the price we are required to pay to enjoy the higher long-term returns historically available in common stock investing. Prudent investing, however, does involve trying to reduce idiosyncratic risk — that is, reducing the risk inherent in the ownership of individual securities. This objective can be pursued in any and all of three ways:

1. The most common way to reduce the risks unique to an individual common stock is not to own too much of it. Broad diversification, then, is the first principle of modern portfolio theory.

2. A second way to mitigate the severity of the calamities that frequently befall individual common stocks is to own high quality stocks.

   Just as bondholders try to reduce the probability of their holding bonds that may default by owning high-quality bonds instead of junk bonds, common stock holders can try to reduce the probabilities that they will own companies that may succumb to difficult economic times by owning high-quality, as opposed to speculative, stocks.

3. The third way to reduce the risk associated with the ownership of individual common stocks is to limit the premiums paid for risk factors A (reliability) and B (growth), above. It is a discussion of the rationale and implementation of such a policy that is the primary purpose of this chapter.

PRICE-EARNINGS RATIOS

The absolute level of the price per share of a common stock conveys little information as to whether the stock is high-priced or low-priced. Price per share must be compared to some other per share parameter such as earnings per share, book value per share, sales per share, or cash flow per share. When making such comparisons we come up with such ratios as the price-to-earnings ratio, price-to-book ratio, price-to-sales ratio, and price-to-cash flow ratio. All may be useful in making judgments about the risk inherent in the price level of a common stock, but by far the most common, and arguably the most useful, is the price-earnings ratio (P/E) which is defined as the price per share of a common stock divided by the earnings per share of the underlying company. In short, a $20 stock selling at 40 times earnings is generally considered to be higher priced than a $40 stock selling at 20 times earnings.

THE EFFICIENT MARKET HYPOTHESIS

The efficient market hypothesis (EMH) asserts that the current price of a common stock is the best measure of the value of that stock that can be arrived at by any means known to man. In other words, the current price of a stock measures, and evaluates *accurately*, a company's viability and reliability, its potential for growth, and the value the financial markets should ascribe to these factors at any instant in time. As a faithful subscriber to the EMH, I personally accept these conclusions.

What the EMH does not, and cannot, address, however, is our own personal and individual tolerances for risk. As owners of common stocks we most easily address our tolerance for risk by owning broadly diversified portfolios of high quality securities. In this regard, however, it may also be useful to limit our exposure to risk by limiting our exposure to stocks with unusually high price-earnings ratios.

RELATIVE PRICE EARNINGS RATIOS (RP/E)

An important tool for assessing the vulnerability of a stock to an idiosyncratic collapse of its price-earnings ratio is a measure known as its *relative* price-earnings ratio (RP/E). The RP/E of a stock is its actual P/E divided by the P/E of the average stock (most commonly the average in the Standard & Poor's 500 Stock Index). If the average stock has a P/E of 20, a stock with a P/E of 10 has an RP/E of 0.50, a stock with a P/E of 20 has an RP/E of 1.00, a stock with a P/E of 30 has an RP/E of 1.50, and a stock with a P/E of 40 has an RP/E of 2.00.

The beauty of the RP/E is that it controls for the overall level of the market. In other words, though we can argue that a stock should have a higher P/E today than it had a decade or two ago because the price level of all stocks is higher, this argument does not apply to the RP/E. The fact that we have been in an extended bull market since 1982 provides no justification for a stock's RP/E to be above average today. Only idiosyncratic factors can account for such a premium.

We can make judgments about the RP/E of a particular common stock in either or both of two ways:

PREMIUM (OR DISCOUNT) TO THE MARKET

If a stock sells at an RP/E of 1.50, we say that it sells at a 50% premium to the market. It presumably sells at such a premium because its future profitability is regarded as more reliable than that of the average company and/or its profits are expected to grow more rapidly than those of the average company.

In terms of risk, we can argue that, if the company were, all at once, to be perceived as having no more reliability and growth potential than that of the average company, it should immediately lose its 50% premium and so decline by one-third in price in the marketplace.

Similarly, if a stock sells at an RP/E of *less* than 1.00, it is presumably because its future profitability is regarded as *less* reliable than that of the average company and/or its profits are expected to grow *less* rapidly than those of the average company.

PREMIUM (OR DISCOUNT) TO THE PAST —
THE RELATIVE RELATIVE PRICE-EARNINGS RATIO (RRP/E)

We may also compare a company's current RP/E to its median[1] RP/E for some arbitrarily selected period in the past[2]. If, for example, a stock has sold at a median RP/E of 1.20 over the past fifteen years and today it is selling at an RP/E of 1.80, we can say that it is selling at a 50% premium to its past. (1.80 is 50% greater than 1.20). If, then, the profits of this company were once again perceived to be no more reliable and/or promising than they were in the past (but still greater than that of the average company), the 50% premium to the past should disappear (the RP/E would return to 1.20), in which case the stock could lose one-third of its value.

To relate a stock's current RP/E to its historical RP/E over some arbitrarily selected period of time, we shall use here the term "*relative relative* price-earnings ratio (RRP/E)." A stock's RRP/E, then, is its current RP/E divided by its median RP/E over some period of time in the past. In our example above, the stock's RRP/E would be 1.50 (1.80/1.20).

Some further examples of the calculation of RP/Es and RRP/Es appear in the following table:

| | CURRENT | MEDIAN | CURRENT | CURRENT |
Example	P/E	RP/E	RP/E	RRP/E
Average Stock[3]	20x	1.00x	1.00x	1.00x
Stock A	10x	1.00x	0.50x	0.50x
Stock B	20x	0.80x	1.00x	1.25x
Stock C	30x	1.25x	1.50x	1.20x
Stock D	40x	1.60x	2.00x	1.25x
Stock E	50x	1.25x	2.50x	2.00x

A RATIONALE

The ultimate return to a more typical P/E, either in terms of the market as a whole, or in terms of a company's historical past, should be regarded as more the norm than the exception.

Companies do enjoy spurts and sometimes extended periods of growth, and it is these periods that growth stock investors seek to exploit. Most industries and companies, however, at some point, also go through periods of consolidation and retrenchment and sometimes attain maturity or go into decline. Such periods for individual companies are frequently the consequence of competitive factors, even in industries that continue to grow dynamically.

The real question is not *if* a common stock is apt to return to a more normal relative price-earnings ratio but, rather, *when* it is apt to return to such a ratio. Because this question of *when* is a question of market timing and so, at least in this writer's belief, impossible to answer, the best way we have to protect ourselves against the devastation that can be wrought by the collapse of abnormally high relative price-earnings ratios is not to have too large commitments in stocks with such ratios.

THE NIFTY FIFTY OF THE 1970s

For those of us with memories of the debacle of the "Nifty Fifty" in the first half of the 1970s, the risk inherent in abnormally high price-earnings ratios is very vivid indeed.

The Nifty Fifty was a collection of the most popular growth stocks of the late 1960s and early 1970s. These stocks were the favorites of institutional investors and often referred to as "one-decision" stocks, meaning that one purchased them to hold forever because it was believed that the only direction in which they could go was up.

The Nifty Fifty were large capitalization stocks with, for the most part, very high price-earnings ratios. At the peak of their popularity in December of 1972, their average relative price-earnings ratio was 2.22. A list of the Nifty Fifty is provided in the table on page 49.

Also provided in the table is the depth of decline that each of the Nifty Fifty experienced between its high and its subsequent low during the 1970s. It will be noted that, while the market as a whole declined 48%, the Nifty Fifty declined an average of 62%.

The difference between seeing 62% of one's wealth disappear, as opposed to seeing 48% disappear, may not seem all that great. It is useful to note, however, that, for any set of numbers, the component below the average must be as great as the component above the average. In other words, to arrive at an average decline of 48%, there must have been another group of stocks during the 1970s, which we shall call the "Not-So-Nifty" Fifty, that declined, on average, only 34% (the average of 62% and 34% is 48%). Clearly it would have been significantly better during the 1970s to have owned the fifty that were not so nifty.

Let us carry this argument one step further. In examining the Nifty Fifty table, we determine that, while the decline of the 25 stocks with the lower P/Es averaged 57%, the decline of the 25 with the higher P/Es averaged 67%. To arrive at our average decline of 48% for the S&P 500, given that half the Nifty Fifty declined an average of 67%, there must have been a comparable component of our "Not-So-Nifty" Fifty that declined only 29%. Once again, losing 29% of one's wealth is considerably less painful than losing 67%.

The implication would seem to be that, at least in this earlier period, *relative* price earnings ratios were a pretty good measure of the idiosyncratic risk — the risk over and above the risk inherent in the market as a whole — associated with stocks with inordinately high price-earnings ratios.

CONCLUSION

For anyone eager to try to avoid the type of magnified stock market carnage that characterized holders of especially high P/E stocks during the first half of the decade of the 1970s, I suggest examining carefully the RP/Es, and especially the RRP/Es, of the stocks in one's portfolio.

THE NIFTY FIFTY OF THE 1970S

#	Company	P/E	RP/E	% Decline in Early 1970s
1	American Express	37.7x	1.99x	-75%
2	American Home Products	36.7	1.94	-46
3	American Hospital Supply	48.1	2.54	-66
4	AMP	42.9	2.27	-61
5	Anheuser-Busch	31.5	1.67	-70
6	Avon Products	61.2	3.24	-87
7	Baxter Laboratories	71.4	3.78	-61
8	Black & Decker	47.8	2.53	-53
9	Bristol-Myers	24.9	1.32	-63
10	Burroughs	46.0	2.43	-52
11	Cheesebrough Ponds	39.1	2.07	-71
12	Coca-Cola	46.4	2.46	-70
13	Digital Equipment	56.2	2.97	-63
14	Disney (Walt)	71.2	3.77	-86
15	Dow Chemical;	24.1	1.28	-27
16	Eastman Kodak	43.5	2.30	-62
17	Emery Air Freight	55.3	2.93	-68
18	First National City	20.5	1.08	-59
19	General Electric	23.4	1.24	-60
20	Gillette	24.3	1.29	-69
21	Halliburton	35.5	1.88	-47
22	Heublein	29.4	1.56	-73
23	International Business Machines	35.5	1.88	-59
24	International Flavors & Fragrances	29.2	1.54	-60
25	International Telephone & Telegraph	15.4	0.81	-82
26	Johnson & Johnson	57.1	3.02	-46
27	Kresge (S. S.)	49.5	2.62	-64
28	Lilly (Eli)	40.6	2.15	-46
29	Louisiana Land & Exploration	26.6	1.41	-70
30	Lubrizol	32.6	1.72	-50
31	M. G. I. C. Investment	68.5	3.62	-94
32	McDonald's	71.0	3.76	-72
33	Merck	43.0	2.28	-54
34	Minnesota Mining & Manufacturing	39.0	2.06	-53
35	Penney (J. C.)	31.5	1.67	-65
36	PepsiCo	27.6	1.46	-68
37	Pfizer	28.4	1.50	-59
38	Philip Morris	24.0	1.27	-50
39	Polaroid	94.8	5.02	-91
40	Proctor & Gamble	29.8	1.58	-44
41	Revlon	25.0	1.32	-52
42	Schering	48.1	2.54	-53
43	Schlitz (Joe) Brewing	39.6	2.10	-80
44	Schlumberger	45.6	2.41	-47
45	Sears Roebuck	69.1	3.66	-66
46	Simplicity Patterns	50.0	2.65	-90
47	Squibb	30.1	1.59	-65
48	Texas Instruments	39.5	2.09	-58
49	Upjohn	38.8	2.05	-71
50	Xerox	45.8	2.42	-73
	Average	41.9x	2.22x	-62%
	Standard & Poor's 500[4]	18.9x	1.00x	-48%

Sources: Standard & Poor's and *Stocks for the Long Run*, 2nd edition, Jeremy J. Siegel

Chapter 3 Footnotes:

[1] The *median* is used in lieu of the *average* because of occasional outlier P/Es which would tend to distort the average more than the median. For example, a company for which average annual P/Es typically clustered around 20-to-1 over a period of years might have experienced a long strike in one year causing its P/E in that year to average 100-to-1. While use of the 100-to-1 figure might considerably inflate the *average* P/E over that period, it would probably have a negligible effect on the *median* P/E over the same period.

[2] Value Line provides the average RP/E for each of the past 16 years for most of the companies it covers; hence, where available and appropriate, medians for periods of up to 16 years may conveniently be used as a benchmark.

[3] Note that, by definition, the Median RP/E, the Current RP/E, and the Current RRP/E of the average stock are always 1.00.

[4] The S&P 500 peaked at 119.87 on 1/5/73 and had declined to 62.34 on 10/4/74.

4

THE MOTHER OF ALL HEDGE FUNDS AND THE EFFICIENT MARKET HYPOTHESIS

On Friday, August 21, 1998, the world's most prestigious hedge fund, Long-Term Capital Management (LTCM), virtually collapsed, ultimately resulting in its investors' losing over 90% of the capital they had put into it.[1]

Though accepted as established fact by many, for investors needing further evidence of the validity of the "efficient market hypotheses" (EMH), the saga of LTCM provides an excellent example.

Contents

THE EFFICIENT MARKET HYPOTHESIS

The efficient market hypothesis is a theory, based upon countless scientific studies, of how the securities markets work. It states that, because information relating to factors affecting security prices and markets is transmitted to, and assimilated by, investors and potential investors so rapidly, the price of any security or level of any market, at any time, almost instantly reflects any and all publicly available information about that security or market.[2]

Corollaries of the efficient market hypothesis include the following:

1. Nobody, with a consistency greater than that of random chance, can successfully time short-term price moves in either securities markets or individual securities.

2. A strategy of trying to exploit mispricings in securities (buying issues that appear to be undervalued and selling issues that appear to be overvalued) is futile.

3. Anomalies or "free lunches" in the securities markets do not exist.

4. Nobody, over time, can outperform the market sector in which he invests[3].

5. Aside from matters of efficiency,[4] incremental return in investing is achieved by, and only by, taking on added uncertainty or sacrificing safety.

6. We prosper as investors by *participating* in markets, not by trying to *outwit* them.

WHAT IS A HEDGE FUND?

Let us suppose we have $100,000 and we want to create our own hedge fund. It is not a difficult task.

First, we take $50,000 and buy, or "go long," the common stocks of a number of companies that we think should do relatively well in the marketplace. Then, with our other $50,000, we sell "short" a number of companies that we think will do relatively poorly in the marketplace.

(A "short" sale involves selling a security we do not own, borrowing the security from somebody else to deliver to the party to whom we sold it, and planning to repurchase the security to replace our borrowed security at a lower price at some time in the future. If we sell at $50 per share, and repurchase later at $40 per share to "cover" our short sale, we make $10 per share on the pair of transactions. Brokerage firms readily accommodate short sellers by locating lenders of securities that need to be borrowed.)

As we can see, we are now "hedged" against moves in the market. We are "market neutral." If the market goes down, in theory, we gain on our short sales what we lose on our long positions; and, if the market goes up, we gain on our "longs" what we lose on our "shorts."

Though we may now be insulated from moves in the market, if we are to make any money, it must be by outperforming the market — by buying stocks that go up more than the market when the market goes up and/or go down less than the market when the market goes down, and by selling short stocks that go down more than the market when the market goes down and/or go up less than the market when the market goes up.

Though this is the basic theory of a hedge fund, money managers have found numerous other innovative ways to implement the theory. We can hedge with bonds, instead of with stocks. We can hedge with derivative securities. We might, for example, buy call options on a group of stocks we think should do better than the market, and buy put options on a group of stocks we think should do worse than the market.

Hedge funds also engage in arbitrage transactions. As an example, suppose that Company A is selling at $30 per share and Company B is selling at $50. Company B announces that it will make a tender offer for all of the shares of Company A and will give Company B shares in exchange for Company A shares on a one-for-one basis. Company A shares immediately jump in price to $45 per share. The $5 shortfall represents mostly the risk associated with the possibility that the merger will never materialize.

A hedge fund might seek to exploit this $5 shortfall by buying the shares of Company A and selling short an equal number of the shares of Company B. If the deal *goes* through, the hedge fund makes the $5 per share profit. If the deal *falls* through, and the price of Company A stock goes back to $30, the hedge fund loses $15 per share. If the odds of consummation of the merger are better than 3-to-1, the hedge is a good one.

Of great importance, too, hedge funds typically use borrowed money to leverage their bets.

LTCM'S CREDENTIALS

What makes the story of LTCM so instructive is that it probably represented the greatest congregation of human intelligence and financial expertise ever assembled for the purpose of outwitting the markets.

LTCM was the brainchild of John Meriwether who had made a name for himself trading bonds at Solomon Brothers. At Solomon, Meriwether had recruited a Harvard Business School professor, Eric Rosenfeld, who, in turn, had recruited a Harvard economics professor and a professor of finance at the University of California at Berkeley.

Meriwether next brought on board two Nobel Laureates. One was another Harvard Business School professor, Robert Merton, who was noted for his expertise in risk management. The other was Myron Scholes, who had been a professor at both the Massachusetts Institute of Technology and the Stanford Graduate School of Business. Scholes won his Nobel prize in economics in part based upon his model for the pricing of derivative securities.

It was these six former Solomon employees who started LTCM; and, as the fund was getting organized, it was joined by David Mullins, a former Harvard Business School professor, former assistant Treasury secretary for domestic finance, and then vice chairman of the Federal Reserve Board.[5]

LTCM was born in late 1993. It continued to attract financial and mathematical experts (often referred to as "rocket scientists") and, at one point, counted 25 Ph.D.s on its payroll.

LTCM'S CLIENTS

In addition to having a group of the world's most talented financiers to manage its assets, LTCM attracted a collection of extremely sophisticated investors who obviously had enormous faith in the capabilities of these managers. The founding principals themselves had put up a total of $100 million and now a minimum investment of $10 million was required of each new participant.

Among LTCM's domestic clients were PaineWebber with $100 million of its own capital committed, the CEO of PaineWebber with $10 million, the CEO of Bear Stearns with $13 million, Merrill Lynch with $15 million of its own capital and $1.5 billion which it raised from other investors.

Among LTCM's overseas clients were the Dresden Bank of Germany, the Bank of Italy (with a $100 million investment), and several Swiss banks (one of which lost $650 million).

THE KINDS OF BETS LTCM MADE

An example of one of LTCM's early successful trades was its purchase of $2 billion 29½-year U.S. Treasury bonds and the short sale of $2 billion 30-year Treasury bonds to exploit what it concluded was an unwarranted spread between the prices of the two securities. LTCM did not care whether interest rates went up and forced all bond prices down or interest rates went down and forced all bond prices up. It was "market neutral" or "hedged" against such uniform price moves in the bond market. It sought merely to take advantage of the historically wide spread between the prices of the two securities. As these prices converged, and because LTCM borrowed so heavily to finance the transaction, the fund made a $25 million profit, in a relatively short period of time, on an investment of only $12 million of its own capital.

LTCM used takeover arbitrage, as explained above. It dealt in Danish mortgage bonds; it bought Norwegian currency, the krone, and sold the German mark short; it took positions in emerging markets and bond futures; and it made simple bets on the direction markets would move, including a bet that German interest rates would rise.

It was ultimately Russia's default on its debt and the collapse of the Russian ruble that was the undoing of LTCM. The fund had taken a large long position in Russian bonds and a large short position in U.S. Treasuries at a time when the yield spread between the two was historically very wide. It assumed that the spread could only narrow. It did not narrow. It widened still further in what is characterized as a global "flight to safety" or "flight to quality." This led to LTCM's massive losses on August 21, 1998 and fatal margin calls in the days immediately thereafter.

LTCM'S PERFORMANCE

LTCM formally began trading in February 1994 and, in that year, earned 19.9% for its investors, net of expenses. It earned 42.8% in 1995, 40.8% in 1996, and 17.1% in 1997. By late 1998, however, the original LTCM investors had lost over 90% of their capital.[6]

Ignoring the 1998 wipeout, let us put just LTCM's *good* years in tabular form and compare them with the returns on stocks over that period:

YEAR	LTCM	STOCKS
1997	17.1%	33.4%
1996	40.8%	23.1%
1995	42.8%	37.4%
1994	19.9%	1.3%
Average	30.2%	23.8%

Source: Ibbotson 1998 Yearbook: Stocks = S&P 500

To have outperformed stock investors during its first four years in existence surely led to celebration by LTCM managers and investors alike.

LTCM'S USE OF LEVERAGE

In addition to the unprecedented pool of talent that LTCM had to manage its portfolio, the fund had an even more powerful tool. It had the leverage of borrowed money. It borrowed enormous amounts of money from financial institutions all over the world. In fact, it borrowed so much money that it was able to leverage its bets by as much as 50-to-1. As reported in the *New York Times*:

> Long-Term Capital Management used its $2.2 billion in capital from investors as collateral to buy $125 billion in securities, and then used those securities to enter into exotic financial transactions worth $1.25 trillion.

What might we have done with a little bit of leverage in the stock market during the heydays of LTCM? For every dollar we put up of our own, current Federal Reserve regulations permit us to borrow as much as another dollar to purchase stocks. This is called buying stocks on margin. By thus leveraging our bet 2-to-1, we could have earned nearly twice the rate indicated in the "Stocks" column of the previous table.[7] Had we taken on the risk of leveraging our bet 50-to-1, our returns would have been nothing short of spectacular.

Allowing for interest paid on our debit balances at the rate of 10% per year, let us see what opportunities we missed under each of the scenarios:

YEAR	LTCM LEVERAGED UP TO 50-TO-1	STOCKS LEVERAGED 2-TO-1	STOCKS LEVERAGED 50-TO-1
1997	17.1%	56.8%	1,203.4%
1996	40.8%	36.2%	678.1%
1995	42.8%	64.8%	1,407.4%
1994	19.9%	-7.4%	-433.7%
Average	30.2%	37.6%	713.8%

As can be seen, while LTCM was averaging a return of 30.2% per year in its four good years with leverage that ranged up to 50-to-1, we could have averaged 37.6% per year, net of interest, in the stock market with leverage of just 2-to-1; and we could have averaged 713.8% per year, net of interest, if we had leveraged ourselves 50-to-1, as did LTCM.

As we have probably heard many times before, financial leverage is a two-edged sword. While it can work in our favor when all goes according to plan, it can be unmerciful, and financially fatal, when the world does not evolve as we predict. For LTCM, in 1998, the markets clearly did not behave as its mathematical models indicated they should.

REFLECTIONS OF ANOTHER NOBEL LAUREATE

The following is the final paragraph of the *Wall Street Journal* article drawn upon for most of the factual material on LTCM used herein:

> Through it all, LTCM's rise and fall proved what some of those economics professors who stayed on campus had been saying all along: The market is brutally efficient. "Most of academic finance is teaching that you can't earn 40% a year without some risk of losing a lot of money," says Mr. Sharpe,[8] the former Stanford colleague of Mr. Scholes. "In some sense, what happened is nicely consistent with what we teach."

CONCLUSION

Why have hedge funds been responsible for so much hype in recent years? Perhaps they have appealed to the elitism of the super-rich, and perhaps they have been the envy of the not-so-rich. In the last analysis, however, they are little more than Rube Goldberg vehicles for earning less-than-market rates of return and/or for getting clobbered in the securities markets.

LTCM should help teach us the following:

[1] No investor should ever expect to outperform the market sector in which he invests; nor should he ever expect to be able to employ professionals who can do it for him, no matter how brainy those professionals may profess to be.

[2] Strategies which, on their surface, appear to offer something for nothing invariably have, ticking within them, time bombs, of which even their practitioners may be unaware.

There is an old stock market adage that seems a propos in the case of LTCM:

The bulls make money and the bears make money but the pigs go broke.

Chapter 4 Footnotes:

[1] Most of the information herein on LTCM is taken from the lead story in the Wall Street Journal of November 16, 1998.

[2] If the information is not yet in the public domain, and so not yet incorporated into the price of a security, it is "insider" information and so illegal to act upon. Given the enormous scale upon which hedge funds operate, and the severity of the consequences of being caught, it is inconceivable that any such professionally managed fund as LTCM would ever so much as contemplate trading on inside information.

[3] It is also comforting to note that, if nobody, over time, can outperform the market in which he invests, neither can he *under*perform. By definition, the performance of a market is the average of all those who outperform and those who underperform. If there are no *out*performers, then, mathematically, there can be no *under*performers.

[4] The *efficiency* of investing can be enhanced by not paying for services that add no value to the investment process — owning one's securities outright, rather than via the intermediary of a mutual fund or a variable deferred annuity, for example.

[5] According to the WSJ, at a meeting to woo an investor, "Mr. Mullins explained that, because he once was the Fed's vice chairman, he was in the 'heads' of the Fed members and could 'figure out' what they would do."

[6] Based upon the figures provided, and assuming that an investor reinvested his earnings each year, his net return over the life of the fund was -94.4%.

[7] An average investor, fully margined, should have netted twice the total return on the S&P 500, less the interest on the money borrowed.

[8] William F. Sharpe won the 1990 Nobel Prize in Economics for his work in the area of portfolio analysis and management.

5

"GROWTH" VERSUS "VALUE" INVESTING

Contents

INTRODUCTION

There has been an ongoing debate for many years as to whether higher stock market returns can be achieved by investing for "growth" or by investing for "value." Investing for "value" means purchasing stocks at relatively low prices, as indicated by low price-to-earnings, price-to-book, and price-to-sales ratios, and high dividend yields. Investing for "growth" results in just the opposite — high price-to-earnings, price-to-book, and price-to-sales ratios, and low dividend yields.

"Growth" investors are more apt to subscribe to the "efficient market hypothesis" which maintains that the current market price of a stock reflects all the currently "knowable" information about a company and, so, is the most reasonable price for that stock at that given point in time. They seek to enjoy their rewards by participating in what the growth of the underlying company imparts to the growth of the price of its stock.

"Value" investors put more weight on their judgments about the extent to which they think a stock is *mispriced* in the marketplace. If a stock is *underpriced*, it is a good *buy*; if it is *overpriced*, it is a good *sell*. They seek to enjoy their rewards by buying stocks that are depressed because their companies are going through periods of difficulty; riding their prices upward, if, when, and as such companies recover from those difficulties; and selling them when their price objectives are reached.

Which strategy shows the better returns depends, in part, upon the periods over which they are compared. It has, however, been my impression, over the past several decades, that "value" investing has received the more hype. It is the purpose of this chapter to set the record straight.

PERFORMANCE AND SAFETY IN INVESTMENTS

One of the most fascinating aspects of the current mutual fund craze is the buying public's utter disregard for the *quality* of the investments in the portfolios of the mutual funds it acquires. It is almost universally accepted that, if Fund A has gone up more than Fund B over some period of time, it is a better managed fund. *How* that performance was achieved tends to take a back seat to the performance numbers themselves.

How performance is achieved, however, can be of critical importance. The reason it can be important is that the stock market is fickle and, when it falls apart, it falls apart without warning. If a portfolio has achieved its performance by owning high-risk securities (e.g., small, less liquid companies with large amounts of debt, operating in highly cyclical, rapidly changing, or highly competitive industries) and/or using high-risk strategies (e.g., derivative securities such as options, futures, or warrants), it is not well-prepared for those difficult times which unexpectedly rock the securities markets about every quarter of a century or so.

PREMIUMS FOR SAFETY

Let us recognize that we are naturally predisposed to pay a premium for safety. We stop and look both ways before we cross the street, in spite of the extra expenditure of time and energy it requires. We carry fire insurance on our houses, in spite of the improbability that our houses will burn down, and in spite of the many other things we might otherwise enjoy with all the money we pay for insurance premiums.

United States Treasury Securities are considered to be the world's safest investments. But securities of *agencies* of the United States Government cannot be far behind. Federal Land Bank, Federal Farm Credit Bank, Federal Home Loan Bank, Federal Home Loan Mortgage, and Federal National Mortgage Association bonds all carry Moody's ratings of Aaa. The former are considered safer because they are "legal" obligations of the United States Government, whereas the latter are only "moral" obligations of the United States Government. (The solvency of the Federal Deposit Insurance Corporation which insures our bank accounts, for example, is backed by a "moral," as opposed to a "legal," obligation of the U.S. Government.)

I ask my reader to contemplate a scenario in which the United States Government fulfills its obligations to pay interest and principal on its legal obligations but permits the obligations of its federal agencies (including FDIC insurance) to default. This, it would seem, would need to be an event more catastrophic than our republic has yet experienced, and certainly an event more serious even than the Great Depression of the 1930s.

Nevertheless, the marketplace pays a premium to own U.S. Treasuries, as opposed to Federal Agency bonds. A glance at the *Wall Street Journal* reveals that, for comparable maturities, bond buyers are willing to sacrifice between ½ of 1% and 1% in yield to own the former, rather than the latter. As improbable as it is that the incremental safety afforded by Treasuries over Federal Agencies will ever be needed, investors are willing to pay a substantial premium (sacrifice in yield) to own them.

The same situation exists with municipal bonds. In spite of the fact that the general obligations (GOs) of a state are backed by the taxing power of all of the assets within that state, Aaa state GOs yield less than Aa state GOs.

The differential between Aaa corporate bonds and Aa corporates provides still another example. The sacrifice in yield required to own a Aaa corporate versus a Aa corporate is of the order of ½ of 1%. Again, imagine the economic or monetary scenario in which Aaa corporate America meets its obligations, but Aa corporate America defaults.

Given that municipal bonds are considered less safe than U.S. Government bonds, that corporate bonds are considered less safe than municipal bonds, and that a company's common stock is always less safe than its weakest bond, should we not expect that the marketplace might be willing to pay a premium for *safety* (as well as for appreciation potential) in a common stock?

The important principle to understand is that, given two common stock portfolios, A and B, if Portfolio A is made up of higher quality issues — companies less apt than those in Portfolio B to go bankrupt in a period such as the Great Depression of the 1930s, the Great Credit Crunch of the 1970s, or an economic/monetary scenario more catastrophic than has yet been experienced — then, barring the occurrence of such a catastrophic event, and all other things being equal, Portfolio A should show a *lesser* return than Portfolio B. Portfolio A must pay an insurance premium for its added protection against catastrophic events, as improbable as their realization may seem. It should expect to pay this premium by accepting lesser total returns, in the absence of a catastrophic event.

NEW MORNINGSTAR DATA

The Morningstar mutual fund service is the most popular and most comprehensive of all the mutual fund rating services. Beginning in late 1996 and early 1997, the service modified the way it categorized mutual funds. Common stock funds are now divided into nine groups, according to whether they invest in large capitalization, medium capitalization, or small capitalization companies, and whether their investment styles are predominantly "growth" oriented, "value" oriented, or a "blend" of the two. For the first time, this data gives us an opportunity more easily to study, compare, and contrast the collective character of the portfolios, and the performance records, of large numbers of mutual funds using "growth" and "value" stock approaches as their investment strategies.

The data used for this analysis covers over twelve-hundred mutual funds with over $½ trillion in assets. Morningstar makes such an analysis relatively easy because it publishes a page for each investment style which it calls an "Overview." On this page is a listing of the twenty-five largest holdings of all the mutual funds in each sector, the relative size of each position, and the collective performance data for the funds in that sector. By examining the quality of the twenty-five largest holdings of the mutual funds in a sector, we can get a pretty good picture of the character of the portfolios in that sector.

MEASURING THE QUALITY AND SAFETY OF LARGE-CAP PORTFOLIOS

The most popular, and probably the best, way to measure the safety of a common stock is to look at its Standard & Poor's rating. Standard & Poor's rates most large capitalization stocks, and a portion of the universe of mid-cap and small-cap stocks, on a scale of A+, A, A-, B+, B, B-, C, and D. These ratings are in no way meant by Standard & Poor's to be prognostications of performance in normal markets. They are meant more to serve as measures of the degrees of protection available in each security in a *catastrophic* market.

Based upon the twenty-five largest holdings in the collective portfolios of the large capitalization "growth" and large capitalization "value" sectors, a profile of each sector appears in the following table:

	S&P QUALITY RATING AT OR ABOVE		
LARGE-CAP STYLE	A+	A	A-
Growth	29.5%	34.4%	42.6%
Value	19.0%	22.8%	32.6%

An alternative measure of the ability of a company to withstand economic and/or monetary adversity can be found in its Value Line "financial strength" rating. This is essentially an assessment of the company's balance sheet. Value Line's rating scale is as follows: A++, A+, A, B++, B+, B, C++, C+, and C.

A breakdown of the financial strength ratings for the large-cap "growth" and "value" portfolios appears in the following table:

	VL FINANCIAL STRENGTH RATING AT OR ABOVE		
LARGE-CAP STYLE	A++	A+	A
Growth	37.5%	61.2%	86.4%
Value	13.7%	45.2%	73.3%

The implication appears to be that, at least for large capitalization portfolios, the quality is conspicuously higher, and so the safety significantly greater, in "growth" style portfolios than in "value" style portfolios.

Such a finding should not be surprising. "Growth" stocks represent companies that are currently thriving, while "value" stocks commonly represent companies in trouble. That is why the prices of the former are high and the prices of the latter are low. Companies that are thriving are apt to be in better shape to confront catastrophic conditions than are companies already in trouble, even before a catastrophe occurs.

Let us state again, however, that, for this incremental quality and safety, "growth" investors should expect to pay some price — such as the acceptance of a lower total return on their portfolios in normal times than they might enjoy if they were to sacrifice some of their quality and safety as in "value" investing.

MEASURING THE QUALITY AND SAFETY OF MID-CAP AND SMALL-CAP PORTFOLIOS

Standard & Poor's ratings are less useful for measuring the quality and safety of mid-cap and small-cap portfolios because there are so many such companies that Standard & Poor's does not rate at all. In contrast, the universe of securities given "financial strength" ratings by Value Line is about twice as large as the universe rated by Standard & Poor's.

A look at the relative "financial strength" ratings of "growth" and "value" mid-cap portfolios is provided in the following tabulation:

VL FINANCIAL STRENGTH RATING AT OR ABOVE					
MID-CAP STYLE	A++	A+	A	B++	LOWER OR NR*
Growth	10.3%	24.6%	38.5%	73.7%	26.3%
Value	0.0%	16.1%	27.9%	50.5%	49.5%
*NR= Not Rated					

Again, the evidence seems quite persuasive that mid-cap "growth" stock portfolios are generally of higher quality, and so would be better able to withstand catastrophic economic conditions, than would a typical "value" portfolio.

In the case of small-cap portfolios, the quality difference is far less pronounced. While small-cap "growth" portfolios were 28% invested in companies with B++ or better Value Line financial strength ratings, the small-cap "value" portfolios were 27% invested in this category. This is not surprising, however, since it is unlikely that *any small*-capitalization companies, whether "growth" or "value," would be very well insulated from the havoc of a catastrophic economy. Size alone confers some degree of comfort.

THE SO-CALLED "INVESTMENT ANOMALIES"

Investment strategists and writers frequently refer to what they call "investment anomalies." These are investment strategies that seem to show higher rates of return than they should, based upon the risks taken.

"Value" investing itself — investing in low price-earnings ratio stocks — and investing in small capitalization stocks are said by some to be anomalies. Another popular strategy said to produce anomalous results is investing in the "Dogs of the Dow." This approach involves creating a portfolio out of the ten highest yielding stocks of the thirty stocks in the Dow-Jones Industrial Average and readjusting the portfolio annually, selling and buying to make sure the portfolio again conforms to the criterion of representing the ten highest yields in that index. A further refinement of this strategy consists of owning only the five lowest priced issues of the ten highest yields in the Dow. Investment trusts have even been marketed to implement the strategy for us. When the "Dogs of the Dow" strategy is back-tested over *limited* periods of time (and especially periods of declining interest rates), it produces rates of return that exceed those that would have been earned by owning all thirty stocks in the Dow-Jones Industrial Average.

The logic is flawed in most such comparisons, however. One cannot compare "apples to oranges." If one is going to own stocks with the lowest price-earnings ratios, stocks of the smallest companies, stocks with the highest yields, or stocks with the lowest prices, almost by definition, one is also going to own the stocks of companies most apt to go bankrupt in a catastrophic economy — an economy where Aaa bonds prove their worth over Aa bonds, where U.S. Treasuries meet their obligations but Federal agencies default, and where our savings account is salvaged only because our bank is FDIC-insured.

It surely would not be considered an *anomaly* to discover that investors (or speculators) made more money by investing in high-risk securities in stock market periods where high-quality was not needed. The owners of "junk" bonds may get higher returns on their bonds than the owners of high-quality bonds — as long as we do not have a serious recession or Great Depression. This is not considered an anomaly. Similarly, the possibility that owners of "junk" stocks might get higher returns than owners of high-quality stocks (as long as we do not have a serious recession or Great Depression) would come as no surprise.

To return to our insurance analogy: All other things being equal, the owner of an income-producing apartment building will earn a higher net return if he does *not* carry fire insurance on his building than if he *does* — as long as he does not have a fire, which he probably will not have. Such an observation, however, can hardly be construed as the discovery of an anomaly.

THE RECORDS OF PERFORMANCE

The inference, so far, is that, because "growth" investors enjoy greater protection against such perils as another Great Depression, they should expect, and should be satisfied with, lesser rates of return in normal times than those presumably enjoyed by "value" investors. To compare the rates of return of higher-quality "growth" portfolios with the rates of return of lower-quality "value" portfolios, in normal times, as we have said, is to compare "apples to oranges."

Though it may appear that "growth" investors *should* be content with lesser returns than those enjoyed by "value" investors, before reaching the conclusion that they actually *do* receive lesser returns, let us examine the following data — again from Morningstar:

RELATIVE ANNUALIZED 10-YEAR TOTAL RETURNS			
COMPARISON	LARGE-CAP	MID-CAP	SMALL-CAP
Growth vs. Value	+2.85%	+2.79%	+2.95%
Growth vs. Blend	+1.67%	+0.98%	+1.84%

As can be seen, whether the "growth" strategy is compared against the "value" strategy or a "blend" of "growth" and "value" strategies, over the past ten years, the "growth" strategy has produced the higher returns. Furthermore, depending upon whether we are looking at small-cap, mid-cap, or large-cap portfolios, this outperformance of "growth" over "value" or "blend" strategies has ranged from nearly 1% to nearly 3% per year.

AN IMPORTANT NOTE

In spite of the fact that we are using the abundant data made available by mutual funds and a mutual fund rating service to demonstrate the advantages of a "growth" investment strategy over a "value" investment strategy, I do not want our readers to conclude that I am endorsing investment in mutual funds that pursue "growth" strategies or any other strategies. Nothing could be farther from the truth.

Without belaboring the point here, let us simply note that, though "growth" funds appear to outperform "value funds, not one of the nine groups of mutual funds examined here even matched the Standard & Poor's 500 over the past ten years. The degrees of underperformance ranged from a low of 0.69% per year for small-cap "growth" funds to a high of 3.64% per year for small-cap "value" funds. As a general rule, domestic mutual funds *underperform* the markets in which they invest by about 3% per year, while foreign and international funds *underperform* their markets by about 4% per year. That is to say, mutual funds underperform *randomly selected* and *unmanaged* portfolios by these 3%-to-4% amounts, every year, year-after-year. Direct investment in common stocks is clearly the more efficient way to invest.

DO GROWTH STOCK INVESTORS GET A FREE LUNCH?

The foregoing data imply the paradox that "growth" investors both earn higher rates of return and enjoy greater safety than do "value" investors. "Growth" investors, however, do not really get a free lunch. They make two sacrifices. First, they must accept a greater part of their investment returns in the form of less predictable *capital gains*, as opposed to more predictable *dividends*. A comparison of the dividend yields currently available for the various styles of mutual fund investing appears in the following table:

DIVIDEND YIELD			
STYLE	LARGE-CAP	MID-CAP	SMALL-CAP
Growth	0.3%	0.2%	0.1%
Blend	1.1%	0.6%	0.4%
Value	1.7%	1.2%	0.8%

It is important to realize that the performance figures presented in the earlier section are "total return" figures which *combine* both capital appreciation and dividends. The nature of the sacrifice made by "growth" investors illustrated in this last table is not in the *amount* of money they receive, but rather in a greater uncertainty as to *when* they receive it.

The apportionment of returns between dividends and capital gains for each of the nine mutual fund sectors over the past ten years appears below:

% OF TOTAL RETURN FROM DIVIDENDS VERSUS CAPITAL GAINS (1986–1995)

STYLE	GROWTH		BLEND		VALUE	
Capitalization	Dividends	Capital Gains	Dividends	Capital Gains	Dividends	Capital Gains
Large	10.2%	89.8%	19.1%	80.9%	24.4%	75.6%
Medium	5.7%	94.3%	13.1%	86.9%	20.1%	79.9%
Small	2.6%	97.4%	7.4%	92.6%	10.9%	89.1%

On the basis of the foregoing data, it appears that "value" investors derived 11% to 24% of their rewards from dividends, and 76% to 89% from capital gains; "growth" investors, on the other hand, derived only 3% to 10% of their rewards from dividends, with 90% to 97% coming from capital appreciation.

The second sacrifice "growth" investors experience, in normal times, is a greater volatility in their portfolios. It is simply characteristic of high price-to-earnings ratio stocks that their day-to-day, week-to-week, month-to-month, and year-to-year price swings tend to be more violent than those of low price-to-earnings ratio stocks. The magnitude of this volatility is commonly captured in a yardstick called "Beta." "Beta" is a measure of the historical volatility of a stock or a portfolio, relative to the market as a whole. The market is defined as having a Beta of 1.00; stocks and portfolios that are *more* volatile than the market have Betas of *greater* than 1.00, and those *less* volatile than the market have Betas that are *less* than 1.00.

Morningstar provides the average Betas for each investment style, as reproduced in the following table:

AVERAGE BETA (VOLATILITY)			
STYLE	LARGE-CAP	MID-CAP	SMALL-CAP
Growth	1.02	1.04	0.98
Blend	0.94	0.90	0.82
Value	0.91	0.85	0.66

It appears from the foregoing that "growth" investors probably experience from 10% (in large caps) to 50% (in small caps) more volatility in their portfolios than that experienced by "value" investors.

These two sacrifices — having to accept more erratic capital appreciation in lieu of periodic dividend income, and having to accept greater volatility in the value of our principal — may be summed up in an esoteric concept called "equity duration." Duration is a term most commonly applied to bond investing as a measure of the sensitivity of the price of a bond to a change in interest rates. If, however, we define "duration" in more general terms as "a measure of the degree of uncertainly in the timing of our rewards," "growth" stocks tend to be "longer duration" investments than "value" stocks and so capitalism must pay us more to put up with them.

CONCLUSION

In summary, it appears that "growth" investors enjoy higher total returns than do "value" investors, and that they also have greater protection against calamitous events such as depressions, credit crunches, and other catastrophes such as we can only imagine. For these benefits, however, growth investors must be willing to accept a greater portion of their total returns in the form of irregular capital gains, as opposed to more regular dividends; and they must be willing to accept higher short-term volatility in the values of their portfolios.

INDEXING

Contents

INTRODUCTION

Indexing involves maintaining a portfolio of *all* of the securities in a market index in the same proportions as they are weighted in the index and, thereby, enabling one's own portfolio precisely to track that index. The most common index that investors seek to track is the Standard & Poor's 500.

Investors often ask, how can I make sure that I track the S&P 500, if my portfolio is not large enough to hold 500 stocks, and in the proportions held by the index?

The answer, of course, is that one cannot *exactly* track the S&P 500, if one does not own *exactly* the S&P 500 portfolio. There seems to be a pessimistic, but erroneous, supposition by indexers, however, that, if they do not index, they will necessarily *underperform* the market in which they invest. But not tracking the S&P 500 *exactly* is not the same as doing *worse* than the S&P 500. If one has a cross-section of the S&P 500, the odds are exactly as good that he will do *better* than the S&P 500 as that he will do *worse* than the S&P 500.

Tracking the S&P 500 with *precision* can hardly be a worthwhile investment objective in itself. As an analogy, let us assume we want to drive from New York to Los Angeles but do not want to get lost. We might chose to follow somebody else who is making the same trip and knows his way. If asked what our "objective" was, we would say "to get to LA," not "to follow another driver." Clearly, if there were some better way not to get lost, it would be worthy of investigation.

If one does, nevertheless, see emulating the S&P 500 as a goal, and he can *approximate* its performance, with no greater chance of doing worse than of doing better, then he had ought to be content. This, however, is an objective easily attainable with far fewer than 500 stocks. Historically, for example, the Dow-Jones Industrial Average, made up of only 30 stocks, has served as an excellent proxy for the S&P 500. In fact, the coefficient of correlation between the Dow-Jones-Industrial Average and the S&P 500, over the 73-year period between 1926 and 1998, is 99.7%; and the coefficient of correlation between the total returns (meaning dividends reinvested) on the two indices is 99.8%.

THE PURSUIT OF PORTFOLIO QUALITY

One of the ways of hedging some of the risk in common stock investing is to own high-quality common stocks. The presumption is that, if we have a catastrophic economy and a catastrophic stock market, larger companies with strong balance sheets and in less cyclical industries will be more apt to survive than small companies with weak balance sheets and in highly cyclical industries.

In financially catastrophic times, it also goes without saying that the bonds of any individual company would also prove a more viable investment than the common stock of that same company. In addition to the relative safety of bonds over stocks, however, bond investors usually give considerable consideration to the quality of the individual bonds they own. Great deference is shown among bond investors to the ratings accorded bonds by the rating services. If bonds are rated AAA, AA, or A by Standard & Poor's, they are considered of high quality; if they are rated BBB, they are considered of medium quality; and, if they are rated BB or lower, they are regarded as "junk" bonds.

With so much attention given by bond investors to the quality of the specific bonds in their bond portfolios, in spite of the fact that the bonds of any company are always safer than the common stock of the same company, it intrigues me that more attention is not given by common stock investors to the quality of the specific stocks in their stock portfolios.

Standard & Poor's quality ratings for common stocks are as easily obtained as are its bond ratings for bonds; and its scale of letter grades is similar. Common stocks of above-average quality receive letter grades of A+, A, or A-; stocks of average quality receive a B+; and stocks of "junk" quality receive a grade of B or lower.

Getting back to indexing: By definition, the quality of half the stocks in the Standard & Poor's 500 are above the average quality of the stocks in the index, and half are below the average quality of the index. In fact, at any given time, about 40% of the stocks in the index are rated A+, A, or A-; about 20% are rated B+; and the remaining 40% either are rated B or lower or are not rated at all.

Furthermore, as indicated above, given that the common stock of any company is always less safe than the lowest quality bonds of that same company, it would seem even more important to be concerned about the quality of the common stocks in one's common stock portfolio than the quality of the bonds in one's bond portfolio.

If, then, one wants to maintain a portfolio of stocks of above-average quality, he must cast out from consideration about 60% of the stocks in the S&P 500.

THE POTENTIAL FOR PORTFOLIO PERFORMANCE

The same argument against indexing can be used if one attempts to discriminate, as most investors do, among common stocks on the basis of their ability to perform in the marketplace. Again, by definition, for any period in the future, as they have for all periods in the past, half the stocks in the index deliver an *above-average* performance, while the other half deliver a *below-average* performance.

Though there can be no disagreement about which stocks were above average and which were below average in the past, there is always considerable debate over which will be above-average performers and which will be below-average performers in the future.

To address this question, however, here are at least two useful guidelines:

[1] Generally, the common stocks of companies which have enjoyed high rates of return on equity and which have retained a high proportion of their earnings for reinvestment in their own operations have shown higher total returns in the marketplace than have the stocks of companies with low returns on equity and which, in addition, have paid out in dividends a larger part of what they earned.

Again, by definition, half the companies in the S&P 500 Index fall into each of these two groups; hence, if one wanted to own those in the former group only, he would need summarily to cast out half the stocks in the index.

[2] Generally, companies with above-average Value Line "Timeliness" ratings have delivered significantly higher future rates of total return than have companies with below-average Value Line "Timeliness" ratings. Because above-average Value Line "Timeliness" ratings usually reflect above-average earnings growth in the underlying companies, these ratings are commonly used as a proxy for helping to identify growth companies.

At any given time, approximately one-quarter of the stocks in the S&P 500 have above-average Value Line "Timeliness" ratings (#1 or #2); approximately half have neutral ratings (#3); and about one quarter have below-average ratings (#4 or #5). Hence, if one wants to maintain an above-average portfolio, insofar as Value Line "Timeliness" ratings are concerned, one would need, again, to be sure that he excluded from ownership about three-quarters of the issues in the S&P 500.

One measure of the potential for improving portfolio performance by discriminating among the types of stocks owned is provided by Morningstar mutual fund service which provides the following data:

AVERAGE ANNUAL TOTAL RETURN FOR PERIODS ENDING DECEMBER 31, 1998

	1 Year	3 Years	5 Years	10 Years
Growth Funds	35.75%/yr.	25.91%/yr.	20.61%/yr.	18.46%/yr.
Value Funds	12.34%/yr.	19.74%/yr.	17.88%/yr.	15.53%/yr.
Difference	23.41%/yr.	6.17%/yr.	2.73%/yr.	2.93%/yr.

Clearly, over the past decade, there has been some performance benefit to investing in the "growth" stock sector of the common stock universe.

INDEXING WITH MUTUAL FUNDS

It would appear that indexing with mutual funds or with variable annuity sub-accounts is even less advantageous than indexing with a portfolio of common stocks. Not only is one denied the opportunity to modify either the quality of his portfolio or its potential for growth, but he is also burdened with a built-in performance handicap or "efficiency shortfall," as documented in the following table:

AVERAGE ANNUAL TOTAL RETURN FOR PERIODS ENDING DECEMBER 31, 1998			
SERIES	1 Year	3 Years	5 Years
Standard & Poor's 500 Composite	28.34%/yr.	28.15%/yr.	24.02%/yr.
Mutual Funds Indexed to S&P 500	27.41%/yr.	27.12%/yr.	23.10%/yr.
Shortfall	0.93%/yr.	1.03%/yr.	0.92%/yr.
Variable Annuities Indexed to S&P 500	26.69%/yr.	25.88%/yr.	21.83%/yr.
Shortfall	1.65%/yr.	2.27%/yr.	2.19%/yr.
SERIES	10 Years	15 Years	20 Years
Standard & Poor's 500 Composite	19.13%/yr.	17.78%/yr.	17.63%/yr.
Mutual Funds Indexed to S&P 500	18.29%/yr.	16.45%/yr.	15.95%/yr.
Shortfall	0.84%/yr.	1.33%/yr.	1.68%/yr.
Variable Annuities Indexed to S&P 500	17.09%/yr.	N/A	N/A
Shortfall	2.04%/yr.	N/A	N/A
Source: CDA/Wiesenberger			

As can be seen, the average mutual fund indexed to the Standard & Poor's 500 has underperformed its index by about 1½% per year, and the average variable annuity indexed to the S&P 500 has underperformed its index by about 2% per year.

The sources of these shortfalls include the administrative expenses associated with operating the fund, as well as "market impact" costs associated with the buying and selling of securities necessary to track changes in the index and to accommodate investor cash flows into and out of the fund. "Market impact" costs are the price penalties to which institutional investors are subject by virtue of the large blocks of stock they must trade when they buy or sell.

A chronic 1½% or 2% per year performance shortfall may seem less burdensome in a stock market that has delivered average annual rates of return in excess of 20%. If and when the markets revert to their more typical 10% to 12% rates of return, and after adjusting for taxes and inflation, however, 1½% or 2% deducted from one's total return, year-after-year, can detract considerably from the after-tax, inflation-adjusted return one earns on his money over a long span of time.

ANOTHER ANALOGY

Indexing may be compared to trying to duplicate the lifestyle of the Joneses. We might try to do everything the Joneses do — no more, no less. When the Joneses paint their house green, we paint our house green; when they buy a new car, we buy exactly the same kind; and, when they take a trip to the Caribbean, we take one also, at the same time and for the same duration. We forgo the possibility of having an experience more gratifying than any the Joneses have in an effort to minimize the possibility of having an experience less gratifying than any they have. As copycats, however, we are never quite able to keep up with the Joneses. They get their house painted and their car purchased before we know what they are up to; and they get a better price on their tickets to the Caribbean because they are able to purchase them farther in advance. Such is the lot of the indexer, as the data in the foregoing table and a mountain of other evidence so clearly demonstrate. In an effort not to underperform, the indexer pursues mediocrity, foregoes the opportunity to outperform, and, in the process, of necessity, underperforms, nevertheless.

By definition, half of all common stock investors who try, will outperform the average. Endeavoring merely to be in the upper half of any competition ought not be regarded as an overly ambitious goal. The indexer, however, even in that modest pursuit, surrenders before he starts.

"LARGE CAP"
VERSUS
"SMALL CAP"
INVESTING

Contents

A DIALOGUE BETWEEN MUTUAL FUND MANAGERS, MOE AND CURLEY

Moe: Where are you guys putting your money these days?

Curley: We are investing quite heavily in the second half of the alphabet, especially those companies beginning with the letters "S" through "Z." What are you folks buying?

Moe: As you know, the first half of the alphabet has been doing well lately, and so we are sticking with it. We have been underperforming the market at a rate of only 3% per year. "A" through "C" has been on quite a roll.

Curley: I know, but because the second half has been lagging for quite some time, we think it is about ready to move.

Moe: Do you have any explanation as to why various sectors of the alphabet tend outperform others from time to time?

Curley: It is our theory that, in the early stages of a bull market, before investors are fully invested, they look down alphabetical lists of companies and spend all their money before they get very far down their lists; then, as the bull market matures, the prices of stocks in the first half of the alphabet tend to get overpriced and, in looking for bargains, investors tend to discover the latter half of the alphabet, and those stocks begin to move. How do you folks explain it?

Moe: We tend to feel that companies beginning with the early letters of the alphabet probably have more enlightened managements. These managements recognize the higher visibility and better recognition of companies beginning with the early letters, and so change their companies' names, if they are too far down the list. It is probably a pretty prudent move to change your company's name from United States Widgets to American Widgets, for example. A management with the wisdom to make such a change, we feel, is probably wise enough to discover and implement other such critical strategies as well. For this reason, we have a general bias toward the first half, and especially so for the first quarter, of the alphabet. We have been told that, in spite of occasional divergences, over longer periods of time, the first half has tended to outperform the second half.

In the last analysis, however, we do not much care what the rationale of a strategy is. If it seems to work, we use it.

Curley: In assigning companies to alphabetical sectors, we encounter considerable difficulty in figuring out where to put such companies as Liz Claiborne and The Gap. We are constantly debating whether these companies should be classified by their first names or their last names. It obviously makes a big difference whether you are assigned to the Cs or the Ls, or whether you are lumped with the Gs or the Ts.

Moe: I know what you mean. Our staff spends a lot of time researching and deliberating these questions.

Curley: It is, I suppose, because of our ability and dedication in tackling these difficult investment issues that our shareholders are willing to pay us our million dollar salaries. It's a great business, don't you agree?

Personally, I would ascribe little more utility to a discussion of "large cap" versus "small cap" investing than I would to the foregoing dialogue. Let me try to explain why.

CAPITALIZATION DEFINED

The "capitalization" of a company is the product of the current market price of its common stock and the total number of its shares outstanding. If a common stock sells at $25 per share and there are one million shares outstanding, the company is said to have a "market capitalization" of $25 million. Market capitalization is the total worth that the marketplace currently puts on a whole company.[1]

Security analysts and services that maintain stock market indices[2] currently have the universe of common stocks classified in, not just two, but four groups, according to market capitalizations — "large-cap," "mid-cap," "small-cap," and "micro-cap."

The dollar values that distinguish each group are somewhat arbitrary; they are different for different analysts and services; there is considerable overlap; and they have tended to increase over time, as companies have grown and the stock market has risen. For example, the upper limit for inclusion as a "small" capitalization company is now about twice what it was just five years ago.

The stocks in the Standard & Poor's 500 Index are generally regarded as approximating the "large" capitalization sector of the U.S. stock market. These 500 companies range from General Electric with a market capitalization of nearly $200 billion, down to companies with market capitalizations of about $2 billion. Mid-cap companies tend to cluster in the range of $2 billion down to $1 billion, with "small" caps being defined as companies under $1 billion down to $200 million, and micro-caps being everything else that is smaller.

THE RATIONALE FOR CAPITALIZATION CATEGORIES

It has been observed in many studies that, if one divides the common stock universe up into categories based upon market capitalizations, one finds that there are periods when smaller capitalization companies as a group tend to perform better in the marketplace than larger capitalization companies, and vice-versa. In fact, over very long periods of time, smaller capitalization companies seem, generally, to have outperformed larger capitalization companies.

One common inference is that one might try to switch between large- and small-cap stocks as indicated by their expected relative performances and so enhance one's overall investment returns. For those who have less faith in their ability to time such markets, a second inference might be, always, to put a greater emphasis on the ownership of smaller rather than larger cap stocks than one otherwise might.

MARKET CAPITALIZATION AND FIRM SIZE

In discussions regarding large- and small-cap stocks, it is almost universally assumed that market capitalization is a good proxy for firm size. Large capitalization companies, because they are generally larger than small capitalization companies, are presumably *collectively* "safer." It is harder to imagine General Electric, Coca-Cola, or Exxon going bankrupt than it is some smaller company with an unfamiliar name. Conversely, more small capitalization companies than large capitalization companies, because they are generally smaller, have greater potentials for growth. It is clearly easier to imagine a small company's doubling its sales and profits in each of the next five years than it is to imagine General Electric, Coca-Cola, or Exxon doubling its sales and profits in each of the next five years.

I contend, however, if one is attempting to define "safety" in terms of "large corporate size" or "potential for growth" in terms of "small corporate size," market capitalization is somewhat of a tangential and grossly imprecise way to go about it.

There are four common ways of measuring firm size — sales, profits, assets, and market capitalization. Market capitalization is the least logical of the four in that it tells us more about the current price of a company's common stock than it does about the fundamentals of the underlying company.

Market capitalization, because it is a direct function of the price of a company's stock, is, by far, the most volatile of the four measures of company size. If a stock's price doubles in a year, and many do, a company's market capitalization doubles, by definition. It is far less likely, however, that its sales, profits, or assets have doubled over that same period of time. If none of the latter has doubled, can we legitimately argue that the company is, nevertheless, twice as big as it was the year before?

If a stock doubles in price over a short period of time and causes its company to be reclassified from small-cap to large-cap, should one feel safer owning it? After a stock has doubled in price, and its price-earnings ratio has risen nearly as much, most investors would feel the risk of owning it is now greater, not less.

Similarly, if a company falls upon hard times and the price of its stock drops by 50%, in turn, causing it to drop from large-cap to small-cap status, should we construe that event as an indication that we now have a company with greater prospects for growth than it had before its adversity?

In order to see just how poor market capitalization is as an indicator of firm size, let us consider each of the four common yardsticks, one-by-one.

We might chose to define company size in terms of total sales. Those companies with the largest sales are the ones that have the biggest claims on our pocketbooks; they account for the largest shares of the goods and services generated by the nation, as measured by Gross Domestic Product. As seen in the following table, however, only four of the ten largest companies in terms of sales are also among the ten largest in terms of market capitalizations:

RANK BY SALES[3]	COMPANY	RANK BY CAPITALIZATION
1	General Motors	21
2	Ford Motor	35
3	Exxon	3
4	Wal-Mart Stores	11
5	General Electric	1
6	IBM	10
7	Mobil	19
8	Chrysler	66
9	Philip Morris	7
10	AT&T	16

We might define size in terms of profits. It would seem that companies with the greatest profits have the greatest flexibility, clout, and control over their own destinies. They have the greatest ability to pay big dividends, to expand internally, or to make acquisitions. As seen in the following table, however, only six of the ten largest companies, as measured by profits, are also among the ten largest companies when measured by capitalizations:

RANK BY PROFITS	COMPANY	RANK BY CAPITALIZATION
1	Exxon	3
2	General Electric	1
3	Philip Morris	7
4	AT&T	16
5	IBM	10
6	Intel	5
7	General Motors	21
8	Ford Motor	35
9	Merck	6
10	Citicorp	18

We might measure size by total assets. A case can surely be made that those companies controlling the greatest amount of the nation's wealth are really the nation's largest companies. When size is measured by total assets, the disparity is widest of all. Only one of the ten largest companies by assets is also among the ten largest by capitalization. In fact, the ten largest companies, as measured by their assets, on average, rank 50th, in terms of their capitalizations:

RANK BY ASSETS	COMPANY	RANK BY CAPITALIZATION
1	Fannie Mae	32
2	Chase Manhattan	31
3	Citicorp	18
4	General Electric	1
5	Ford Motor	35
6	BankAmerica	34
7	General Motors	21
8	Morgan, J. P.	75
9	Merrill Lynch	94
10	Morgan Stanley	155

If we next look at the ten companies with the largest capitalizations, we find that, depending upon whether we are looking at sales, profits, or assets, these other measures rank the top ten capitalizations anywhere from #1 to #195:

RANK BY CAPITALIZATION	COMPANY	SALES	——— RANK BY ——— PROFITS	ASSETS
1	General Electric	5	2	4
2	Coca-Cola	52	13	151
3	Exxon	3	1	27
4	Microsoft	144	28	195
5	Intel	40	6	104
6	Merck	45	9	100
7	Philip Morris	9	3	42
8	Proctor & Gamble	16	14	83
9	Johnson & Johnson	36	18	123
10	IBM	6	5	30
5.5	Average	36	10	76

INVESTMENT OBJECTIVES, POLICIES, STRATEGIES, AND TACTICS

Investors and portfolio managers have investment objectives which they pursue with various investment policies, strategies, and tactics

Our personal investment objectives are best defined in terms of our individual tolerances for uncertainty. Specification of a desired rate of return is hardly a meaningful investment objective for, in this regard, we are all the same. Who does not desire to maximize his rate of return? Once we have, somehow, established and specified our tolerance for uncertainty, it is the marketplace that will determine our rate of return.

We might next define for ourselves an investment *policy* that accommodates our tolerance for uncertainty. We might, for example, decide that we can live with no more uncertainty than that characterized by a portfolio that is held half in cash and half in common stocks.

Our *strategy* for the cash might be to hold bank certificates of deposit, money market funds, or U.S. Treasury bills. Our *strategy* for common stocks might be to hold high-quality growth companies, aggressive growth companies, cyclical companies, high-dividend paying companies, troubled companies, small companies, large companies, or a combination of any of these. Our *tactics* might determine for us when to be in one group or another.

There are any number of reasons why one might elect to invest in any of these common stock categories or any of many more such categories. There are always legitimate reasons for believing that any of these groups of stocks will be favored in the marketplace during some future period of time. Interest rates may be expected to rise, or to fall; the economy may be expected to expand, or to contract; or the investing public may be expected to become more exuberant or more conservative. Such factors, most assuredly, would affect these different market sectors in different ways.

I am unable, however, to imagine any economic, monetary, or other market scenario that would more likely target a subset of companies defined by their market capitalizations than a subset of companies defined by the size of their sales, their profits, or their assets.

A SIMPLIFIED EXAMPLE

In terms of their *sales, profits,* or *assets,* let us define half of all companies as "large" and the other half as "small."

Let us next recognize that a stock sells at a premium (e.g., a high price-earnings ratio[4]) because of the market's perception that the company is of above-average quality and/or that it has an above-average potential for growth. Let us call such a company one held in *"high* esteem." Similarly, a stock sells at a discount (a low price-earnings ratio) because of the market's perception that the company is of below-average quality and/or that it has a below-average potential for growth. Let us call such a company one held in *"low* esteem."

Because market capitalization is a function of common stock price as well as firm size, it follows that, among the major members of the "large capitalization" category will be (1) all very large companies, including those priced at a *discount* because they are held in *low* esteem and (2) moderately small companies priced at a *premium* because they are held in *high* esteem.

Conversely, among the major members of the "small capitalization" category will be (1) all very small companies, including those priced at a *premium* because they are held in *high* esteem and (2) moderately large companies priced at a *discount* because they are held in *low* esteem.

The following diagram may better help depict the foregoing categories:

SOME MAJOR MEMBERS OF THE LARGE-CAP AND SMALL-CAP STOCK CATEGORIES

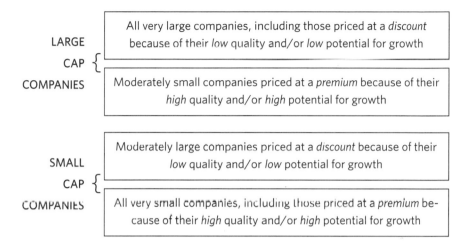

The important point to be made is that some significant number *smaller* companies (as measured by sales, profits, or assets) get thrust into the *large* capitalization category by virtue of their *premium* prices; and, similarly, some significant number of *larger* companies get pushed down into the *small* capitalization category by virtue of their *discounted* prices.

Just how significant the number and magnitude of these dislocations are can be gleaned from the range of the price-earnings ratios (P/Es) of the companies appearing in the preceding tables. They range from a low of 6-to-1 for Chrysler to a high of 48-to-1 for Microsoft. In terms of the market's current perception of quality and potential for growth, Microsoft is held in eight times higher esteem than Chrysler. If Chrysler had the same P/E as Microsoft, it would have a market capitalization eight times as large as it has now. Similarly, if Microsoft had Chrysler's P/E, its market capitalization would be only one-eighth of what it is now. Clearly, the level of a company's price is far more important than the magnitude of its sales, profits, or assets in assigning it a rank on the basis of market capitalization.

What do all very *large* companies held in *low* esteem have in common with moderately *small* companies held in *high* esteem? What do all very *small* companies held in *high* esteem have in common with moderately *large* companies held in *low* esteem? To both questions, I would answer, "not much." If they have little in common, there is no reason to expect them to move in tandem in response to any particular, economic, monetary, or other market dynamics.

Large companies may move together for a number of reasons, the most obvious of which is the safety associated with their large size. Small companies may move together for a number of reasons, the most obvious of which is the greater potential for growth associated with their small size. It is extremely difficult, if not impossible, however, to define a reasonable set of circumstances which would either favor or disfavor both *very large* companies held in *low* esteem and *moderately small* companies held in *high* esteem versus *very small* companies held in *high* esteem and *moderately large* companies held in *low* esteem. Such disparate collections of stocks are not likely to march to the same drummer, no matter what the drummer's beat might be.

That very large companies and moderately small companies selling at premiums may *seem* to move together is easily explained by the fact that, collectively, this particular assemblage of companies is populated more by large companies than by small companies, as measured by sales, profits, and assets; and such large companies may, indeed, logically move together at times. Similarly, the universe of small capitalization companies is populated more with small companies, as measured by sales, profits, and assets, than by moderately large companies selling at discounts, and such small companies, too, may have trends that are independent of, and diverge from, those of large companies at times.

As an analogy, let us suppose that someone makes the observation that he thinks men are more conspicuous in crowds than women. When asked why, he says because men are generally taller than women. Would it not have been at least marginally more useful to make the observation that "tall" people are more conspicuous in crowds, irrespective of whether they are men or women?

DATA MINING

Data mining is the practice of looking at historical data to find patterns and, then, in the absence of a plausible theory to explain the patterns, using them, nevertheless, to make projections into the future. Sunspot cycles and hemline trends have been said to correlate with bull and bear markets in the past, but few people use them productively to manage their portfolios today. It is said that, historically, the best single predictor of the Standard & Poor's 500 Stock Index has been butter production in Bangladesh, but portfolio strategies based upon this correlation have not gained wide acceptance.

Portfolio managers, though they vary widely in their investment strategies, are in near universal agreement that any technique, in addition to appearing to have worked in the past, must have some logical explanation as to *why* it has worked, before they will bet money on its working in the future.

I ask those who engage in the large-cap-small-cap dialogue to explain *why* a group of stocks which have nothing more in common than the size of their market capitalizations should ever respond in unison to any economic, monetary, or other set of market forces and, if so, just what these forces might be.

CONCLUSION

Why, then, is market capitalization so widely used as a measure of firm size? I suspect that it is used by default. Unable to agree whether sales, profits, or assets is the best yardstick, portfolio managers, at least, can compromise with market capitalization. Though they cannot agree on which of the four measures is the *best*, they can all agree on which of the four is the *worst*, and so that is what they use.[5]

For the foregoing reasons, however, it is this writer's opinion that large-cap-small-cap discussions are not useful; and, most assuredly, the large-cap-small-cap dichotomy is not useful for defining an investment objective, policy, strategy, or tactic.

Whether they be mutual fund managers, investment advisors, stock brokers, or individual investors, I believe those defining a focus of their investments in terms of large-cap and small-cap categories are victims of the "Moe 'n' Curley illusion" illustrated in the opening paragraphs of this chapter.

Chapter 7 Footnotes:

[1] Market capitalization is often referred to as the total amount of money one would need to pay to acquire an entire company. Actually, however, somewhat more than its current market capitalization is usually needed to buy an entire company in the open market because, as soon as a potential buyer starts buying shares, he bids up the price of the stock, and so increases the company's total market capitalization. This effect is apparent in the case of takeovers where an acquiring company must offer a premium to the current market price of the stock of a target company when undertaking a takeover of that company.

[2] i.e., Standard & Poor's, Frank Russell Company, Wilshire Associates, and the University of Chicago's Center for Research in Security Prices (CRSP).

[3] Data for all the tables herein are taken from *Forbes* magazine dated April 21, 1997.

[4] "Earnings" is another name for "profits." Other yardsticks by which the relative price level of a common stock is commonly measured include its price-to-sales and price-to-book (total assets minus total liabilities) ratios.

[5] Even if measured by sales, profits, or assets, firm size in the absolute is not necessarily a useful concept. A determination of company size that is useful requires a comparison with other companies in its industry. For example, while annual sales of $1 billion would imply very large size for a manufacturer of apparel, it would imply much lesser size for a grocery store chain.

CONVENTIONAL
WISDOM?

Contents

INTRODUCTION

One of my high school teachers used to proclaim that, as we proceeded with our educations, we progressed from questions of "what" to questions of "why." In the areas of financial and portfolio counseling, there are widely accepted dogmas which I suggest practitioners might more frequently examine by posing questions of "why." In spite of their having come to be accepted as a part of the conventional wisdom of investing, my purpose here is to challenge the logic of the following three doctrines:

[1] That all investors should maintain a *cash* reserve (in a checking or savings account, a money market fund, or Treasury bills), as an "emergency fund," equivalent to three to six months of living expenses, over and above those funds normally held for these expenses, so that they will not have to liquidate other investments for an emergency at a potentially inopportune time.

[2] That one's financial assets should be allocated such that the percentage invested in equities (common stocks) is equal to 100 minus his age.

[3] That, in addition to diversifying the equity portion of his portfolio across industries and companies, an investor should "diversify" his portfolio across asset classes.

In challenging these three "generally accepted principles of investing," it is useful to recognize that there are basically three financial asset classes: *cash, bonds,* and *common stocks.* It is further useful to recognize that the returns on bonds historically, and over longer spans of time, have exceeded the returns on cash, and that the returns on common stocks have exceeded the returns on both cash and bonds. For the period 1926 through 1997, the average annual rates of return on three proxies for these asset classes have been as follows:

ASSET[1]	AVERAGE ANNUAL TOTAL RETURN
Cash	3.8%
Bonds	5.2%
Stocks	11.0%
Source: Ibbotson Associates	

To proceed further with our challenge to the foregoing three dogma, we must also be willing to accept the assumption that, though future rates of return may well differ from the above, over longer periods of time, bonds will probably continue to return more than cash, and stocks will probably continue to return more than either bonds or cash. Just what the future rates or differentials may be is not germane to our discussion here; we need only have faith that meaningful differentials shall probably continue to exist, and in the same order.

Why have these differentials existed in the past, and *why* will they probably exist in the future? The explanation lies in the fact that capitalism is so structured that, the greater the *uncertainty* associated with the *timing* of a *return* for a given asset class, the *greater* must be the *return* available from that asset class. If investors did not reap a higher return for investing in an asset class with greater uncertainty in the *timing* of its returns, they would not put their money into that asset class, and so that asset class would cease to exist[2].

EMERGENCY FUNDS

Though the concept of maintaining a reserve in *cash* as an "emergency fund" is about as ingrained in the American psyche as baseball, motherhood, and apple pie, I believe the reasons usually promulgated for doing so warrant some questioning. Whenever I hear the cash reserve policy advocated I am reminded of the story of a small community with three taxis and a single hack stand located in front of the town hall. The community was a busy one, and the selectmen became frustrated with the frequency with which they could not procure a taxi for themselves because all three vehicles were in service.

In an attempt to solve the problem, the selectmen passed an ordinance requiring that there be at least one taxi waiting at the hack stand at all times, and that a lone taxi not be allowed to leave until another taxi had returned to replace it. For all practical purposes, of course, the town now had two taxis, instead of three.

Just as the selectmen's new ordinance incapacitated one of the town's three taxis, a reserve held perpetually in cash for events that occur infrequently, or maybe never at all, may reduce the efficiency of that part of an investor's assets so held.

At this point it seems useful to address the question of *why* we might be advised to maintain an emergency fund in the form of cash. There are two reasons usually proffered: (1) To provide "liquidity" in the event that cash is needed quickly, and (2) to preclude having to sell other investments at an "inopportune" time.

Liquidity

There are few assets more liquid than stocks and bonds. If one elects to sell a stock or bond today, the normal payout date is three business days hence; if one needs the money sooner, for an insignificant sacrifice in price, one can sell for "cash" or, for a nominal interest charge, one can get a "pre-payment," and so eliminate even the three-day delay. Money can be "wired" from one's account to one's bank as "good funds" for use as cash on the same day requested. A very common way to obtain quick temporary cash is to utilize a "margin" account whereby one borrows against his investment portfolio at a moderate rate of interest. This permits the disbursal of cash in an amount equal to up to half the value of one's portfolio on the day requested, without any need, at that time, to focus on whether to sell, what to sell, or when to sell. One can also have check-writing privileges on his margin account and so, effectively, have instant access to these funds. The "need for liquidity" as a justification for holding assets in the form of cash, as opposed to other financial assets, then, is a fiction.

An Inopportune Time to Sell

Implicit in the contention that one might be forced to sell securities to meet an emergency at an "inopportune time" is the arrogance that one can ever identify an "opportune" time to sell. If one believes he, I, or anyone else will ever know whether, from the point of view of timing the market as a whole or timing one investment in particular, it will be better to sell today, tomorrow, next week, next month, or next year, he is deluding himself with a second fiction.

There is one, and only one, good rule-of-thumb for timing one's investments and disinvestments: One makes investments when one has the money available to make them; and one disinvests when he wants to use the money for something else.

If one needs to sell securities to meet an unexpected emergency, he may end up selling when the market is high, or he may end up selling when the market is low; but he will never know whether the market was high or low until after the fact.

The belief that we can know today whether the market is truly high or low is an illusion. If, two years hence, we see the Dow-Jones Industrials two thousand points below where it is today, we shall, then, know that the market was high today; if, on the other hand, we see the market two thousand points higher two years from now, we shall, then, know that it was low today. Because we cannot sell securities retroactively, we can never know in advance whether a time to sell is opportune or inopportune. If we cannot ever know the answer to a question in time to make a decision, then, it is not useful to make addressing that question a part of our decision making process.

Furthermore, if over a lifetime we must sell securities on a number of occasions to meet unexpected expenses, we shall subsequently learn that sometimes we sold when the market was low and sometimes we sold when the market was high but, as the saying goes, "it will all come out in the wash."

In my financial planning readings on "emergency funds," I came upon the following caveat that amuses me to no end:

> It is important that clients recognize that the money drawn for emergencies from established emergency funds must be replaced as soon as possible to manage future emergencies.

In other words, once the emergency fund is disbursed, there is no longer any emergency fund, and so one needs to liquidate other assets at the time of the emergency, or "as soon as possible" thereafter, to recreate the fund. If one is going to have an emergency fund at all times, then, one is precluded from taking into consideration the "opportuneness" of his sale of other assets to replenish the fund. But this is no different from what he would need to do if he had no cash in an emergency fund in the first place. He must sell his other assets, if, when, and as emergencies arise either to meet the emergency or to replenish the emergency fund.

The Downside of A Cash Reserve

As alluded to earlier, money held in a cash reserve is not as productive as money held in longer-term assets. To use a simple example:

Let us assume that the three to six months of living expenses that we are instructed to hold as cash for an emergency amounts to $25,000, and that we are planning over a twenty-five year time frame. Using the historical data in the table above, the difference between the earnings on $25,000 over twenty-five years when invested at 11.0%, versus being invested at 3.8%, is $276,122. This price, in excess of $¼ million, seems like quite a lot to pay to maintain a $25,000 cash reserve.

All of the foregoing notwithstanding, money that may be needed in the near-term for any purpose should not be put into a tax-deferred retirement account such as a 401(k), and it should not be put into a traditional IRA if one is under age 59½. Funds in a 401(k) may not be accessible at all for an emergency; and funds withdrawn from a traditional IRA before age 59½ may be subject to a 10% penalty tax.

As long as one has his readily accessible financial assets invested in publicly traded, marketable securities (as opposed to limited partnerships or shares of a closely held corporation which are not readily marketable), he should feel they constitute his emergency fund, whether those securities are invested in cash equivalents, bonds, or stocks. Furthermore, if one is over age 59½, even all those marketable securities in his IRA may be considered as part of his emergency fund.

In the final analysis, I have no problem with anybody's maintaining a cash reserve, and in any amount with which he is personally most comfortable. I merely think that the foregoing two reasons, promoted by so many financial advisors, are not appropriate reasons for doing so.

THE ASSET ALLOCATION FORMULA

Of all the prescriptions dispensed by financial advisors, that of investing in equities that percentage of one's financial assets equal to 100 minus one's age must be among the most absurd. About the only thing this formula has going for it is that it is easy to apply. Most people know their own age, and subtracting that number from 100 is not a cumbersome task.

Why the number from which we should subtract is 100, and not 50, 500, or, perhaps, the universal constant of gravitation (6.67×10^{-11}), has not been made clear to me. Nor do I yet understand *why*, from whatever that magic number may be, we should subtract our age, as opposed to our height, our weight, or, perhaps, our Social Security number.

Age as a Criterion

I have great difficulty in understanding why "age" should have much bearing on how one invests his money. The argument, of course, goes that young people can better cope with volatility in their investments because they have more time to allow for a portfolio recovery following a portfolio decline, and so they should own more common stocks than older people should.

There is, however, a countervailing argument. The foregoing conventional wisdom assumes that the only risk for an older person with respect to his investments is that of a decline in their value. It is my experience, however, that older people have more often felt themselves victims of inflation and declines in the *purchasing power* of their investments than declines in the nominal value of those investments.

And who is better able to cope with inflation? A young person whose wages will probably at least track the Consumer Price Index, or an older person who must now live on his accumulated savings?

Inflation has traditionally been addressed with equity investments and not much else; hence, I can see, here, a better argument for an older person to invest more heavily in equities than for a younger person to do so.

Degree of Affluence as a Criterion

Another commonly accepted basis upon which to determine what portion of one's assets are appropriately committed to equities is to relate the decision to one's overall level of affluence. The greater one's personal wealth (his cushion of comfort), presumably, the more tolerant that person will be of volatility in the value of his financial assets.

Except insofar as older people tend to be more affluent than younger people, age is not a consideration with respect to this criterion.

Time Horizon of the Portfolio

In my opinion, by far the most logical and useful standard by which to determine an appropriate allocation of common stocks to a portfolio is the "time horizon" of the portfolio.

If a sum of money is earmarked for a college education scheduled to begin next year, it is probably not appropriate to invest the money in either stocks or bonds. Similarly, the proceeds of the sale of a house which are to be used for the purchase of another house are probably funds best held in an interest-bearing cash account.

Using the "time horizon" criterion, one rule-of-thumb for deciding whether or not it is appropriate to invest a particular sum of money in common stocks is to ask if there is a greater than fifty percent probability that the money will stay invested for more than five years. If the answer is "yes," common stocks may be appropriate. Historically, the probability of experiencing a positive return on money so invested over time spans exceeding five years has been quite high[3].

The time horizons of most investment portfolios tend to be quite long. The time horizon of one's IRAs should probably be considered to be longer than the time horizon of his taxable account. That is because it is usually wiser, in retirement, to deplete completely one's taxable account before withdrawing from his IRA (subject to the minimum withdrawal requirements of the latter), in order to preserve the tax-deferral benefit for as long as possible.

If one is depending upon his portfolio as a source of retirement income, that portfolio should be considered to have a time horizon no shorter than its owner's life expectancy. In the case of the portfolio of a married couple, the time horizon should be no shorter than the life expectancy of the second to die. The life expectancy of a single person, age 65, is 20 years; and the life expectancy of the second to die of two people, each age 65, is 25 years. To the extent that one cares to prepare for the possibility of living beyond his life expectancy, the time horizon for his portfolio is even longer than that derived from the life expectancy tables.

Finally, to the extent that one believes his investment portfolio will outlast himself, to be passed on to his heirs, its time horizon may go far beyond his own lifetime and, for all practical purposes, become infinite.

The time horizon of a portfolio seems a far better criterion for determining how the portfolio should be invested than either the age or affluence of its owner, though the latter two variables may, indeed, help determine the former. Nevertheless, using the time horizon criterion, and the five-year rule-of-thumb, there are relatively few portfolios that are not eligible to be invested predominantly or wholly in common stocks.

DIVERSIFICATION ACROSS ASSET CLASSES

My initial discomfort with the concept of diversifying across asset classes lies in the terminology. Traditionally, allocating one's portfolio among stocks, bonds, and cash has been referred to as "balancing" the portfolio. "Asset allocation" is a more modern and, arguably, more appropriate term.

"Diversification" is a term perhaps better reserved for the deployment of one's assets among different investments in the same asset class and, so, among investments with comparable risk/return profiles. One diversifies a common stock portfolio by purchasing the common stocks of different companies and in different industries, and he diversifies a bond portfolio by purchasing the bonds of different issuers. In the case of municipal bonds, good diversification will probably imply issuers in different parts of the country.

A more descriptive term for what is commonly called "diversification across asset classes" is "hedging." If one holds cash to complement his common stock portfolio, he is not "diversifying" in the traditional sense; he is attempting to "hedge" or mitigate the volatility of returns associated with common stock ownership. If he complements his long-term bond portfolio with some inter-mediate-term or short-term bonds, he is "hedging" against the greater volatil-ity characteristic of long-term bonds. Similarly, if he complements his bond portfolio with common stocks, he may be "hedging" against the erosion of the purchasing power of his portfolio associated with inflation.

The significant difference between "diversification" and "hedging" is that, while diversification implies the addition of investments with similar risk/return profiles in an effort to tame portfolio volatility, "hedging" may imply the acceptance of a lower rate of expected return in exchange for a lesser degree of volatility. Hedging, of course, is a more effective way to reduce the volatility of a portfolio, but it is also a more expensive way of doing it.

This, I believe, is what many investors fail to realize and many financial advisors fail to point out. While diversification within an asset class provides a "free lunch," "hedging" with less volatile assets can be very expensive. As to how expensive, one need only refer to the example previously cited of the more than $¼ million foregone by the individual who hedged the volatility of his portfolio for twenty-five years by holding $25,000 in U.S. Treasury bills instead of in common stocks.

If one can learn to differentiate between "diversification" and "hedging" and recognize that, while "diversification" is free, "hedging" may be expensive, he will have made a quantum leap in understanding the management of money.

CONCLUSION

In the last analysis, to ask our financial advisor how much of an invest-ment portfolio should be held in the form of cash and/or bonds is akin to asking our doctor how much salt we should add to our food. The financially or medically best answer to these respective questions may be that none is best, but as little as possible, in any case. As a result, we will arrive at a level of salt that will help preserve our health, but also preclude our giving up food; and, hopefully, too, we will arrive at a balance among equity and fixed income investments that will permit us, not only to prosper with our invest-ments, but to be comfortable with them as well — or, to use a common cliché, to enable us, not only to eat well, but also to sleep well.

Chapter 8 Footnotes:

[1] As its proxy for cash, Ibbotson uses 30-day U.S. Treasury-bills; as one proxy for bonds, it uses a U.S. Government bond with a maturity of 20 years; and, for large capitalization common stocks, it uses the Standard & Poor's 500 Stock Index for 1957-1997 and the S&P 90 for 1926-1956.

[2] This relative degree of uncertainty is measured for bonds with some precision (and used as a measure of their interest rate sensitivity), and sometimes guesstimated for common stocks, with a tool called "duration." Bonds and common stocks are, therefore, often referred to as "long-duration" assets.

[3] Over the 72-year period 1926 to 1997, 60 (90%) of the 67 five-year holding periods have shown positive returns. Over the 55-year period, 1942 to 1997, 48 (96%) of the 50 five-year holding periods have shown positive returns. (I pray that my reader may find the basis for this "50%-five-year" rule-of-thumb logically and empirically more robust than the "100-minus-age" rule-of-thumb herein disdained.)

MUTUAL FUND
EFFICIENCY
AND PERFORMANCE

Contents

INTRODUCTION

The primary purpose for which mutual funds are acquired and held is for their expected good performance. Mutual funds are said to have "professional" managements which, presumably, provide the potential for investment results better than those that the layman might achieve by selecting his own individual securities and subsequently managing his portfolio himself.

Mutual funds, however, are saddled with two burdens which offset some, all, or more·than, the performance benefits derived from the "professionalism" of their managements. The lesser of these two burdens is routinely measured in a mutual fund's "expense ratio" which includes its management fees, administration and operational expenses, and 12b-1 marketing fees.

MARKET IMPACT COSTS

Still greater burdens imposed upon mutual funds are what are known as "market impact costs." These are concessions in price to which all institutional investors are subject when they buy or sell securities by virtue of the large sizes of the positions they must trade. In addition to being functions of the sizes of their positions, the magnitudes of such concessions also vary with the "liquidity" of the securities traded which, in turn, is related to the "market capitalizations" of such securities. The market impact cost of a mutual fund transaction may vary anywhere from ½ of 1% to 20% of the value of the security traded.

The relative burden of market impact costs on a mutual fund's entire portfolio can be estimated, given the total size of its portfolio, the number of issues in its portfolio, the median market capitalization of the securities in which the fund specializes, and the rate of the fund's portfolio turnover (buying and selling).

PORTFOLIO TURNOVER

If one examines the portfolio practices of mutual funds, one is apt to be astounded by the high rates of turnover characteristic of most.

In 1998, the mutual funds categorized by Morningstar as large-capitalization growth funds had an average annual rate of portfolio turnover of 93%, which is equivalent to an average holding period for the stocks in these portfolios of just 12.9 months. Of particular fascination is the extraordinary rates of turnover of the more active mutual funds. The twenty-five most active growth funds covered by Morningstar in 1998 had portfolio turnover rates that ranged from 215% to 972% and averaged 320%, which rates translate into average holding periods of 24 weeks, 5 weeks, and 16 weeks, respectively

Clearly, the detrimental effects of market impact costs on portfolio performance are exacerbated by such high rates of turnover. In fact, if a mutual fund never made any purchases or sales in its portfolio, it would not have any market impact costs at all. It is partially the recognition of this fact that has spawned the interest in index funds. An index funds sells stocks only to rebalance its portfolio to match the index it is tracking or to meet net redemptions. It purchases stocks only to rebalance or to accommodate cash inflows. As a result, index funds have turnover rates of the order of only 5% or so.

Why, then, do mutual funds indulge in so much self-abuse?

One cynical, but plausible, explanation is that active trading is the mutual fund manager's "raison d'être." If an *inactively* traded mutual fund does well, it may be concluded that the manager's services were superfluous; if it does poorly, the manager will be blamed for inaction. On the other hand, if an *actively* traded fund does well, the manager is a hero; but, if it does poorly, it can be said that the manager at least tried.

There is, however, an even more compelling reason for these high mutual fund portfolio turnover rates. This issue is tax-related and, again, is a burden associated with the nature of the beast. If an investor purchases a mutual fund in a taxable account, he takes on the capital gains tax liabilities for the unrealized gains in the mutual fund portfolio.

For example, assume that an investor purchases $10,000 in the shares of a mutual fund for his taxable account and that these shares have a cost basis to the fund of $6,000. Assume that the market sector in which the fund is invested performs poorly, and a year later the investor's shares are worth only $8,000. Assume, further, that, because of its poor performance, the fund experiences heavy redemptions and/or management decides drastically to alter its investment strategy; it sells securities and realizes $2,000 in capital gains. In this case, the mutual fund investor has a $2,000 *loss* but must pay a tax on $2,000 in *gains*. In short, he must pay taxes on somebody else's gains. He can reverse the injustice only if he sells his shares and realizes his own loss.

Nor is the foregoing example purely academic. It conservatively describes what happened in 1998 to great numbers of investors who had previously purchased shares in emerging market mutual funds. During the course of

1998, the average emerging market fund declined in value by from 40% to 50%. These funds were, indeed, forced to sell large amounts of stock to meet mass redemptions; and, no doubt, they also did some significant portfolio restructuring to adapt to the newly perceived realities of the marketplace.

Large unrealized capital gains, then, are clearly a liability for any mutual fund wanting its shares to be purchased by taxable investors. It is in the marketing interests of funds to keep these unrealized gains reasonably low, and they can do this only by selling securities in which they have gains.

Interestingly, the motivation for realizing gains in a mutual fund portfolio is diametrically opposite to the motivation for realizing gains in a personal portfolio. While the mutual fund manager is motivated to minimize the *unrealized* gains in his portfolio in order to attract new investors, the individual investor is motivated to minimize *realized* gains so as to defer or avoid the capital gains tax.

From a tax perspective for a taxable investor, a mutual fund may be said to function as a "Reverse IRA." Whereas a traditional IRA serves to *defer* the taxes on one's income, a mutual fund serves to *accelerate* the payment of taxes.

It is, of course, after the stock market has had a large rise that the magnitude of unrealized capital gains in mutual fund portfolios becomes an important consideration. It is presumably because the stock market has performed so well over the past seventeen years that mutual funds have had to employ such high turnover rates to keep their unrealized gain problems under control. The continuing severity of this problem, in spite of these high turnover rates, however, is illustrated by the following survey of the 84 large-capitalization growth funds for which the information is provided by Morningstar in the summer of 1999. Unrealized gains in this group of funds averaged 54% and ranged from a low of 19% to a high of 194%.

EFFICIENCY

The "efficiency" or "inefficiency" of a mutual fund portfolio, or the extent to which market impact costs and other expenses detract from its overall performance, may be estimated by comparing the fund's performance with some appropriate market index over some long period of time. For mutual funds invested in common stocks, the most commonly used index is the Standard & Poor's 500.[1] For mutual funds invested in bonds, appropriate bond indices are used.

The performance of an index is generally accepted as equivalent to the performance a layman could achieve by selecting securities of the type in the index at *random* and *never managing* his portfolio thereafter.

The extent to which the burdens of market impact costs and other expenses offset the benefits of professional management in a mutual fund portfolio, then, can be effectively estimated, over time, by the degree to which the mutual fund underperforms the market index for the class of securities in which it invests.

THE MUTUAL FUND PERFORMANCE JINX

There are purported to be over 10,000 mutual funds available to the public for purchase. There are also many hundreds of sponsors, each with a stable of these funds. Each of a sponsor's funds pursues a different investment strategy. At any point in time, and over varying periods of time, merely by the laws of random chance, it is inevitable that some funds will have delivered higher returns than others. Those funds which have delivered the highest returns are given the greatest visibility by the many mutual fund rating services; and they are also the specific funds that their sponsors most heavily merchandise. As a result, massive amounts of money pour into them.

The laws of random chance, however, also indicate that, after a period of above-average performance, a fund will probably return to normalcy at best (referred to by mathematicians as a "reversion to the mean").[2] Furthermore, after an influx of new money, the fund's outlook may be even *less* promising than normal. The formerly successful fund may be more likely than other funds to *underperform*. The source of the underperformance is the exacerbation of "market impact costs" associated with the larger amount of money now under management.[3]

A mutual fund that has been showing a decreasing rate of performance, relative to the market in which it invests, is very likely the victim of this commonplace "performance jinx." In short, the very fact that a mutual fund has done well *before* one acquires it, may be the primary *cause* of its doing poorly *after* he acquires it.

The validity of the mutual fund performance jinx is supported by some fascinating statistics. It appears that the average mutual fund investor experiences a rate of return that is not much over half the rate returned by the mutual fund he owns. The following is an excerpt from an article by Robert

Markman in the December 1998 issue of the *Journal of Financial Planning*:

> The Boston market research firm Dalbar found that between 1984 and 1995 the average stock fund posted a yearly return of 12.3 percent, while the average investor in those funds made just 6.3 percent. Similarly, another study showed that during the period January 1, 1991, through October 31, 1995, the 20th Century Ultra fund posted an official return of 26.5 percent. The average shareholder over that period, however, earned only 16.0 percent.
>
> Numerous other examples abound that illustrate the same phenomenon: due to errors in the timing of purchases and sales, most investors do not reap the reward one would expect from their allocations. We call this phenomenon "wastage."

Given that it is hard to believe mutual fund investors experience little over half the returns delivered by their funds, let us illustrate the above phenomenon with a hypothetical example: In Year 1, mutual fund "Red Hot" is small, has 10,000 shareholders, and returns 35%. As a result of its good performance, Red Hot attracts new money and, in Year 2, has 50,000 shareholders. As a consequence of its larger size, however, the fund delivers only 5% in Year 2. The fund has averaged a return of 20% per year[4] over the two-year period, but the average shareholder in the fund has experienced a return of only 10% per year.[5]

In addition to the shortcomings of the vehicles in which they invest, then, it appears that mutual fund shareholders tend to be burdened with a form of mutual fund "whiplash" related to a misguided timing of their purchases and sales.

THE IRONY OF 12B-1 FEES AND ECONOMIES OF SCALE

The following are some observations, excerpts, and conclusions extracted from a study conducted by Sean Collins and Phillip Mack, published in the September/October 1997 issue of the *Financial Analysts Journal* and titled, "The Optimal Amount of Assets under Management in the Mutual Fund Industry."

The study covered mutual fund expense ratios (not including market impact costs) and the behavior of these ratios with respect to mutual fund complexes and individual product lines with various amounts of assets under management.

In particular, the study covered *all* 533 mutual fund complexes that existed in the United States during the years 1990 to 1994, encompassing assets totaling about $2 trillion at the end of the period. A mutual fund complex is a "sponsor" which may offer anywhere from one to scores of different funds (i.e., the Fidelity or Vanguard funds). The study utilized data provided by Lipper Analytical Services. For all mutual funds in the study, expense ratios averaged 1.2% of assets under management.

With respect to 12b-1 fees, the authors noted the following:

> Some funds also charge 12b-1 fees — named after the SEC rule authorizing them — to pay for distribution costs, such as advertising and commissions paid to brokers. Investment companies assess such fees against their funds' assets. Although typically amounting to only a few basis points a year, 12b-1 fees have been contentious since their inception. Investment companies have argued that these fees help reduce fund expenses over the long run because they can be used to pay for promotions that help fund assets grow more rapidly than they otherwise would. Ferris and Change (1987) and Trzcinka and Zweig (1990), however, found that funds charging 12b-1 fees tend to have higher over-all expenses than other funds. They concluded that funds charging 12b-1 fees are imposing an undue burden on their shareholders.

Of their own study, the authors state:

> The coefficient on 12b-1 fees is significant and of the anticipated sign. The positive sign on this variable confirms earlier findings: 12b-1 fees appear to drive up fund costs instead of reducing them.

With respect to equity mutual funds, the study further notes that funds are experiencing diseconomies of scale in their expense ratios when their size exceeds $600 million to $800 million.

Interestingly, the foregoing study does not even address the problem of "market impact costs" which are clearly an even greater expense to mutual funds than are the more visible costs used in the calculation of their expense ratios.

Nevertheless, on the basis of expense ratios alone, mutual funds invested in common stocks, appear to begin to experience diseconomies of scale as they reach $600 million to $800 million in size.

Furthermore, 12b-1 marketing fees, which help a mutual fund grow in size more quickly, are clearly counterproductive in that they exacerbate the problem of diseconomies of scale, even when considering expense ratios alone. When market impact costs are taken into consideration, of course, 12b-1 fees are even more abusive.

In short, a 12b-1 fee is an added expense imposed upon a mutual fund shareholder to attract more investors to his fund which, in turn, produces for him a lower net return.

MEASUREMENTS OF VALUE ADDED AND EFFICIENCY SHORTFALLS

It goes without saying that, by employing the services of a mutual fund, an investor hopes to achieve a level of performance superior to what he would achieve by selecting securities at random and then never managing his list. To the extent that a mutual fund provides an "above-the-market" level of performance, its professional management is said to "add value."[6] To the extent that a mutual fund fails to provide such performance, it may be said to suffer an "efficiency shortfall."

Unlike its other expenses, a mutual fund's market impact costs cannot be measured with precision, and so they are not reported in the institution's prospectus or sales literature. Their magnitude can, however, be inferred collectively for mutual funds in general from tabulations such as the following:[7]

AVERAGE TOTAL RETURN FOR PERIODS ENDING DECEMBER 31, 1998			
Series	1 Year	3 Years	5 Years
Standard & Poor's 500 Index	28.57%/yr.	28.23%/yr.	24.06%/yr.
All Equity Mutual Funds	9.74%/yr.	14.69%/yr.	13.03%/yr.
Average Annual Shortfall	-18.83%/yr.	-13.54%/yr.	-11.03%/yr.
Series	10 Years	15 Years	20 Years
Standard & Poor's 500 Index	19.21%/yr.	17.90%/yr.	17.75%/yr.
All Equity Mutual Funds	13.79%/yr.	13.34%/yr.	15.28%/yr.
Average Annual Shortfall	-5.42%/yr.	-4.56%/yr.	-2.47%/yr.

Although the Standard & Poor's 500 is the most commonly used measure of the performance of the U.S. stock market, it is sometimes argued that, because this index is so heavily populated with high quality, large capitalization stocks, it may not be an appropriate benchmark with which to compare a mutual fund which may be invested in lower quality, smaller capitalization stocks. The obvious refutation: If one can obtain a higher return by investing in the higher quality companies in the S&P 500, why even consider investing in a lower quality mutual fund?

A similar argument pertains to comparing a mutual fund which may include foreign stocks with the S&P 500 which is made up entirely of U.S. stocks. The refutation here, too, is similar: Why take on the added risks (currency exchange and political) associated with the ownership of foreign securities if one can achieve a higher rate of return by owning only the U.S. stocks in the S&P 500?

If one, nevertheless, wants to compare the performance of equity mutual funds with broader market indices which include lower quality, smaller capitalization companies, the Russell 3000 and the Wilshire 5000 are benchmarks available for that purpose. And, if one wants to compare the performance of mutual funds that invest exclusively in U.S. equities with any of the three above-mentioned benchmarks, that, too, is possible. The data in the following tables provide such additional comparisons.

AVERAGE TOTAL RETURN FOR PERIODS ENDING DECEMBER 31, 1998			
Stock Market Index	1 Year	3 Years	5 Years
Russell 3000	24.14%/yr.	25.84%/yr.	22.26%/yr.
Wilshire 5000	23.45%/yr.	25.24%/yr.	21.78%/yr.
All U.S. Equity Mutual Funds	12.24%/yr.	18.02%/yr.	16.05%/yr.
Stock Market Index	10 Years	15 Years	20 Years
Russell 3000	18.48%/yr.	16.93%/yr.	17.30%/yr.
Wilshire 5000	18.11%/yr.	16.67%/yr.	17.20%/yr.
All U.S. Equity Mutual Funds	15.44%/yr.	14.19%/yr.	15.98%/yr.

AVERAGE ANNUAL SHORTFALL			
All Equity Mutual Funds vs.	1 Year	3 Years	5 Years
Russell 3000	-14.40%/yr.	-11.15%/yr.	-9.23%/yr.
Wilshire 5000	-13.71%/yr.	-10.55%/yr.	-8.75%/yr.
All Equity Mutual Funds vs.	10 Years	15 Years	20 Years
Russell 3000	-4.69%/yr.	-3.59%/yr.	-2.02%/yr.
Wilshire 5000	-4.32%/yr.	-3.33%/yr.	-1.92%/yr.

AVERAGE ANNUAL SHORTFALL			
All U.S. Equity Mutual Funds vs.	1 Year	3 Years	5 Years
Standard & Poor's 500	-16.33%/yr.	-10.21%/yr.	-8.01%/yr.
Russell 3000	-11.90%/yr.	-7.82%/yr.	-6.21%/yr.
Wilshire 5000	-11.21%/yr.	-7.22%/yr.	-5.73%/yr.
All U.S. Equity Mutual Funds vs.	10 Years	15 Years	20 Years
Standard & Poor's 500	-3.77%/yr.	-3.71%/yr.	-1.77%/yr.
Russell 3000	-3.04%/yr.	-2.74%/yr.	-1.32%/yr.
Wilshire 5000	-2.67%/yr.	-2.48%/yr.	-1.22%/yr.

SURVIVORSHIP BIAS

Even the foregoing comparisons appear to understate the collective underperformance of mutual funds because of an analytical handicap called "survivorship bias." This tendency for the data to be skewed in favor of the funds is explained in the following excerpts from an article in the *Wall Street Journal* of May 10, 1999:

Out of Sight: Lagging Funds Mimic Houdini

Now you see the poor-performance record; now you don't.

In a magic trick increasingly popular among mutual fund firms, lagging funds are disappearing. Last year, 387 stock and bond mutual funds were merged out of existence, up 43% from the year before, while fund liquidations claimed another 250, a 37% increase, and the number of vanishing stock funds jumped a steep 74% in this year's first quarter, according to newly compiled figures from the fund-tracker Lipper, Inc.

"There's an increasing tendency to bury the record of an underperforming fund and to merge it" into a better-performing one, says Burton Greenwald, a mutual fund consultant in Philadelphia. Some call it "survivorship bias — it makes the industry look better," adds Louis Stanasolovich, president of Legend Financial Advisors of Pittsburgh.

INFERENCES RELATING TO THE EFFICIENCY OF THE SECURITIES MARKETS

Either of two conclusions may be drawn from the foregoing performance data:

[1] If, as many scholars contend, the securities markets are "efficient"[8] and professionals cannot add value by actively managing a mutual fund portfolio, then, the figures in the above tables labeled "Average Annual Shortfall" represent the sum of the mutual fund industry's reported expenses and market impact costs.[9]

[2] If, however, as most mutual fund managers contend, the markets arc *not* efficient, and so professionals can make enlightened purchase and sale decisions by identifying and exploiting under-priced and overpriced securities, then, the shortfall figures in the above table *understate* the magnitude of the mutual fund industry's reported expenses and market impact costs by whatever value these professional managers add.

The fact that the shortfall figures have been rising over the past twenty years indicates that the mutual fund industry's market impact problems arc becoming increasingly severe. This is not surprising, given the rapid growth in the size of mutual funds and an increase in the rates of their portfolio turnover.

In any event, it appears that the combination of reported expenses and market impact costs, on average, now consumes the mutual fund investor's capital at a rate of no less than 11% per year (and perhaps by as much as 19% per year). Given that the stock market has averaged an annual return of over 20% per year in recent years, even after a substantial "haircut," mutual fund investors have netted over 10% per year. The return sacrificed, then, may not have seemed all that burdensome to most mutual fund shareholders. If, and when, the stock market again generates only the 10% returns it has averaged over the past two-hundred years (or generates negative returns, as it has in many years in the past), an 11% (or 19%) built-in performance shortfall may prove more discomforting.[10]

SUMMARY

Given that the mutual fund industry's performance figures, as published, are extremely poor; given that, because of "survivorship bias," the industry's actual results are even worse than those published; given that, because of misguided timing, most mutual fund investors themselves do little better than half as well as the mutual funds in which they invest; and given that the tax motivations and practices of mutual fund managers are inimical to the tax interests of their shareholders, it appears that such investors are playing with a deck that is stacked heavily against them.

AN ANALOGY BY MOE 'N' CURLEY

Moe, a mutual fund portfolio manager
Curley, a layman investor

Moe: I feel pretty good today. I earned 10% last year on the mutual fund stock portfolio I manage;[11] and I also went canoeing last weekend and covered an average of 10 miles per hour paddling my canoe.

Curley: I do not know much about investing, but I am an avid canoeist. 10 miles per hour is a pretty good paddle. Where did you canoe?

Moe: On the river.

Curley: Upstream or downstream?

Moe: Downstream.

Curley: How fast is the current in the river?

Moe: 29 miles per hour.

Curley: If the current was 29 miles per hour and you were traveling only 10 miles per hour, it sounds to me as though you were paddling backwards at 19 miles per hour.

Moe: Maybe so, but I was paddling very fast.[12]

Curley: Do you realize that, if you were to canoe upstream and paddle backwards at 19 miles per hour, you would be going in the wrong direction at the rate of 48 miles per hour?

Moe: I do not plan to canoe upstream.

Curley: We shall have to talk about investing sometime. I understand that the stock market returned 29% last year.[13]

CONCLUSION

At least one alternative obviously superior to the purchase of common stocks *indirectly* via mutual funds is the *random* selection, *outright* purchase, and *unmanaged* retention of common stocks *directly*, without the mutual fund as an intermediary.

Chapter 9 Footnotes:

[1] During "bull" markets, securities portfolios of lower quality (high risk) might be expected to outperform securities portfolios of higher quality (lower risk); during "bear" markets, the opposite might be expected.

[2] Numerous studies have demonstrated the absence of any positive correlation between the past performance of a mutual fund and its *future* performance.

[3] In recognition of the magnitude the market impact cost burden, many mutual funds have closed their doors to new investors after having reached a certain size. The Fidelity Magellan Fund is a case in point.

[4] $(35\% + 5\%)/2 = 20\%$

[5] $[(1 \times 35\%) + (5 \times 5\%)]/6 = 10\%$

[6] The amount of "above-the-market" value added to a portfolio's total return is referred to by the term "alpha."

[7] The performance data herein is taken from the CDA/Wiesenberger and Morningstar mutual fund services.

[8] Supporters of the "efficient market hypothesis" assert that the price of every security in the marketplace already incorporates, discounts, or reflects all the information known (and that can be legally acted upon) with respect to that security, and so no investor, neither layman nor professional, can outperform the market in which he invests with a probability greater than that of random chance.

[9] Reported operating expenses accounted for only 1.41% of 1998's 16.33% U.S. stock fund shortfall, implying that "market impact costs" accounted for the 14.92% balance. In other words, the costs that were not reported were over ten times as great as the costs that were reported.

[10] As an example, during the decade of the 1970s (1/1/70 to 12/31/79) the average total return on the Standard & Poor's 500 was 5.9% per year. An 11% haircut, then, would have left the mutual fund shareholder with a negative rate of return of about 5% per year for that entire ten-year period.

[11] In 1998, the average stock fund returned 9.74%

[12] In 1998, the average domestic stock fund had a rate of portfolio turnover of 85% which implies an average holding period of 14 months.

[13] In 1998, the stocks in the S&P 500 Stock Index returned 28.57%.

10

A "BARBELL" APPROACH TO ASSET ALLOCATION

INTRODUCTION

Asset allocation is the term used traditionally to describe the apportionment of one's financial assets among the three major asset classes — cash, bonds, and common stocks. In more recent times, the universe of assets among which an asset allocator might allocate a portfolio has come to include a multitude of other products that the investment and insurance communities have created and marketed.

It is my impression that many financial planners approach asset allocation much as some might approach a buffet dinner. If an item is on the table, they should have some, irrespective of whether or not it is good for them, the faith, perhaps, being that, if it were not good for them, it would not be on the table.

It is, then, not uncommon to encounter elaborately and expensively tailored financial plans that include — in addition to common stocks, bonds, and cash — mutual funds, deferred annuities, real estate investment trusts, convertible bonds, preferred stocks, limited partnerships, foreign securities, precious metals, and a multitude of other more complex investment vehicles. There is also computer software which, somehow, will tell us to what extent our portfolio should be deployed in each of these areas.

Outside of stocks, bonds, and cash, it is usually pretty easy to demonstrate that the ownership of any other investment vehicle to achieve legitimate investment objectives, no matter what these objectives may be, is both unnecessary and inefficient. I have written elsewhere on the shortcomings of many of these other vehicles and will be happy to make any such writings available upon request. It is the purpose of this chapter, however, to demonstrate that even the time-honored bond probably falls into this category of investment vehicles that are both unnecessary and inefficient, irrespective of one's investment objectives.

ALTERNATIVE INVESTMENT VEHICLES AS TRADE-OFFS

All investing involves trade-offs. If we acquire Investment #1 for a benefit we want, as opposed to Investment #2 that lacks the benefit, it is an absolute certainty that we are sacrificing some other advantage present in Investment #2 that is not present in Investment #1— whether we are aware of it or not. If the benefit of Investment #1 that we are receiving is of greater value to us than the benefit of Investment #2 that we are sacrificing, Investment #1 is, of course, the more suitable investment for us. One may, for example, legitimately invest his cash in bank certificates of deposit, instead of U.S. Treasury bills, because he considers the psychic satisfaction of dealing with his local bank a greater benefit than the state income tax exemption on the income earned on U.S. Treasury bills.

By far the most important trade-off in investing, however, is what is known as the risk-reward trade-off. If we expose our capital to greater risk, over time and in the aggregate, we are supposed to reap greater monetary benefits.

The monetary benefits in investing are pretty simple to understand and to measure. They come in the form of interest, dividends, and capital appreciation (or depreciation) and are expressed as rates of total return. Risks, however, are a bit more complicated, both to understand and to measure.

"RISK" AND "VOLATILITY" DIFFERENTIATED

The terms "risk" and "volatility" tend to be used interchangeably. I believe this is semantically unfortunate because the term "risk" implies the possibility of a *permanent* loss, while the term "volatility" implies that any consequent loss need be only *temporary*. Understandably, most people are far less uncomfortable contemplating a temporary depreciation in the value of their assets than they are contemplating an outright and irrecoverable loss of those assets.

While volatility is an attribute of an investment, risk is an attribute of both an investment and its owner. An investment that may entail considerable risk for me may entail minimal risk for you. The second variable that needs to be combined with the volatility of an investment to assess its risk to its owner is the owner's "holding period." If the owner's holding period is too short, a given level of volatility may pose for him a great risk; if, on the other hand, his holding period is relatively long, that same level of volatility may pose for him minimal risk.

In the case of a class of investments which fluctuate in value, then, the risk (the probability and magnitude of any permanent loss) is a function both of the *nature* of the investment and the *length* of the owner's holding period.

STANDARD DEVIATION AS A MEASURE OF RISK AND VOLATILITY

In an effort to quantify all three dimensions of risk — (1) probability of loss, (2) magnitude of possible loss, and (3) individual holding periods — mathematicians utilize a concept known as "standard deviation." With respect to rates of return, standard deviation is a measure of the frequency and degree by which the return on an investment varies from its average rate over some period of time — usually one year.

The very definition of "standard deviation" introduces a second semantic difficulty. Standard deviation interprets returns which "vary" *above* the average as equal in significance to returns that "vary" *below* the average. As Mark Twain once remarked, however, "A wife does not so much object to her husband's gambling. She mostly objects to his losing." Standard deviation, which may be described as the mathematical measure of the probable pain in the ownership of an investment, draws no distinction between above-average *profits* and above-average *losses*, yet it is only the latter that cause pain.

A good way to try to understand standard deviation is with some examples: The average return on common stocks over the past seventy years has been about 10% per year, with a standard deviation of 20%. This means that, in very close to two-thirds (68%) of those seventy years, the rates of return on common stocks ranged from between 30% (10% plus 20%) to -10% (10% minus 20%). In one-third of those years, the returns were either greater than +30% or less than -10%.

Similarly, for small capitalization stocks, over the past seventy years, the average rate of return has been about 12% per year, with a standard deviation of about 35% per year. The range of returns in two-thirds of those seventy years, then, has been between +47% (12% plus 35%) and -23% (12% minus 35%). In one-third of those years, the returns were either greater than +47% or less than -23%.

Over long spans of time, the correlation between the rates of return and the standard deviations of asset classes and market sectors has been extremely good. In general, the higher the standard deviation of returns on an asset class, a market, a market sector, or an investment vehicle, the higher has been the rate of return on that particular investment category.

In structuring our portfolio of financial assets, the most critical question we have to address is what degree of volatility in the income on, and value of, our assets we are willing to tolerate. The greater the volatility we are willing to endure, the greater the return, over time, we should expect to earn on our money. Similarly, our tolerance for volatility should be enhanced as we increase the length of our intended holding period for the investment or class of investments being evaluated. And, as noted above, in spite of its shortcomings, the best measure we have, and the universally accepted measure of volatility is standard deviation.

HOW TO ADJUST STANDARD DEVIATION FOR HOLDING PERIODS OTHER THAN ONE YEAR

In one of our previous examples, we said that, over the past seventy years, common stocks have delivered an average rate of total return of about 10% per year with a standard deviation of about 20% per year. If we use this data to look forward, we might say that, on average, in two years out of three, we should expect a return on our common stocks that lies between -10% and +30%; while, in the other year, we should expect a return that is either greater than 30% or less than -10%.

Notice, here, that both total return and standard deviation are annualized. The unit of time, or holding period, is one year. If we want to assess the probability of a big gain or a big loss over some longer (or shorter) period of time, we may use the following formula:

$$\text{Standard Deviation for N Years} = \frac{\text{Standard Deviation for 1 Year}}{\sqrt{N}}$$

Note: For the mathematical perfectionist, the following more complex formula is the more precise, in that it allows for annual compounding, while the simpler formula above does not:

$$\text{SD for N Years} = \frac{\log(1 + \text{SD for 1 Year})}{\sqrt{N}}$$

If, for example, we want to calculate the standard deviation of investing in stocks over a *five-year* holding period, we simply divide the standard deviation for one year by the square root of five (about 2.2) as follows:

$$\text{Standard Deviation over 5 Years} = \frac{20\%}{\sqrt{5}} = \frac{20\%}{2.2} = 9\%$$

The more precise formula above will produce 8.2% vs. 8.9% with the simpler formula.

This means that, if our expected holding period is five years, the range of our expected average returns in two-thirds of such five-year holding periods should be within the range of +19% per year (10% plus 9%) and +1% (10% minus 9%). In two-thirds of all five-year holding periods, we should earn less than 19% per year but more than 1% per year; and, in the other-third of all those five-year holding periods, we should earn more than 19% or less than 1% per year.

HISTORICAL DATA

In the following table, I have reproduced the average annual rates of total return and standard deviations for cash, bonds, and common stocks over various periods from five to seventy years. The figures are calculated from the seventy years of data found in the publication, *Stocks, Bonds, Bills, and Inflation 1996 Yearbook,* published by Ibbotson Associates — the most widely used source of data for studies such as this. The proxies for cash, bonds, and stocks used here are 30-day U.S. Treasury bills, 20-year U.S. Government bonds, and the Standard & Poor's Composite Stock Index, respectively.

HISTORICAL RATES & VOLATILITIES OF RETURNS ON CASH, BONDS, & STOCKS							
		CASH		BONDS		STOCKS	
Thru 1995 From	Length of Period	Avg. Annual Total Return	Standard Deviation	Avg. Annual Total Return	Standard Deviation	Avg. Annual Total Return	Standard Deviation
1926	70 years	3.7%	3.3%	5.2%	9.2%	10.5%	20.4%
1946	50 years	4.8%	3.2%	5.3%	10.5%	11.9%	16.6%
1966	30 years	6.7%	2.6%	7.9%	12.3%	10.7%	16.4%
1971	25 years	7.0%	2.8%	9.6%	12.5%	12.2%	16.6%
1976	20 years	7.3%	3.0%	10.4%	13.6%	14.6%	13.7%
1981	15 years	7.1%	3.1%	13.5%	13.8%	14.8%	13.6%
1986	10 years	5.6%	1.8%	11.9%	12.2%	14.8%	13.8%
1991	5 years	4.3%	1.2%	13.1%	14.7%	16.6%	15.7%

As the first row of data in the foregoing table indicates, over the past seventy years, the average annual total return on U.S. Government bonds has been 5.2% per year, while the standard deviation for these bonds over the period has been 9.2% per year. This means that, in one-third of these seventy years, the rate of return on U.S. Government bonds has been either greater than 14.4% (5.2% plus 9.2%) or less than -4.0% (5.2% minus 9.2%). How, one might ask, does one earn a *negative* rate of return on a U.S. Government bond?

The explanation as to how the total returns on a U.S. Government bond can be so volatile, and so frequently negative, is that the price of any bond fluctuates with interest rates. When interest rates go way down, the value of a long-term bond goes way up; and, when interest rates go way up, the value of a long-term bond goes way down. Total return is the sum of the interest payments plus appreciation or minus depreciation. If the deprecation of the value of a bond exceeds its interest payments in a given year, the total return for that year will be negative, just as it would be negative for a stock in a year when its value declined by an amount that exceeded its dividend payments.

Though it received far less publicity, prior to the stock market crash of October 1987, the bond market had crashed in April of 1987. In spite of the stock market crash in that year, however, the average common stock holder enjoyed a net gain in 1987, while the average long-term bond holder experienced a net loss in that year. It is, then, the high volatility of their prices, caused by the high volatility of interest rates, that makes the total returns on long-term bonds so volatile.

BARBELL BONDS

The basis for arguing that bonds are both unnecessary and inefficient in an investment portfolio is the observation that, at least over the past seventy years, it has been possible historically to construct a portfolio out of common stocks and cash that has had (1) the same return as a bond portfolio but less risk (volatility as measured by standard deviation), (2) the same risk as a bond portfolio but a greater return, or (3) *both* a greater return and less risk than that of a bond portfolio. I call these synthetically constructed bonds "barbell bonds," made up of varying proportions of cash on one end and stocks on the other.

A set of computations demonstrating how it has been possible, by blending cash and stocks, to equal the returns on U.S. Government bonds, with less portfolio risk than holding bonds, appears in the following table:

RISKS OF BARBELL BONDS VS. U.S. GOVERNMENT BONDS WITH EQUAL RATES OF RETURN							
			BARBELL BONDS			U.S. GOV. BONDS	S/D OF BARBELL BONDS
Thru 1995 From	Length of Period	Required Return	% Cash	% Stocks	Standard Deviation	Standard Deviation	as % of S/D of U.S. Gov. Bonds
1926	70 years	5.2%	78%	22%	7.1%	9.2%	77%
1946	50 years	5.3%	93%	7%	4.1%	10.5%	39%
1966	30 years	7.9%	70%	30%	6.7%	12.3%	55%
1971	25 years	9.6%	50%	50%	9.7%	12.5%	78%
1976	20 years	10.4%	58%	42%	7.5%	13.6%	55%
1981	15 years	13.5%	17%	83%	11.8%	13.8%	86%
1986	10 years	11.9%	32%	68%	10.0%	12.2%	82%
1991	5 years	13.1%	28%	72%	11.6%	14.7%	79%

The most dramatic example we note in the foregoing table is that, over the past half century, it has been possible, with a portfolio that was 93% in cash and only 7% in stocks, to match the total return on U.S. Government bonds but with only 39% as much risk as with holding only U.S. Government bonds.

The following table uses the same data, but assumes that portfolios of cash and stocks are created which duplicate the *risks* (standard deviations) as in the bond portfolios.

RATES OF RETURN ON BARBELL BONDS VS. U.S. GOVERNMENT BONDS WITH EQUAL RISK							
			BARBELL BONDS			U.S. GOV. BONDS	T/R OF BARBELL BONDS
Thru 1995 From	Length of Period	Maximum Std. Deviation	% Cash	% Stocks	Avg. Annual Total Return	Avg. Annual Total Return	as % of T/R of U.S. Gov. Bonds
1926	70 years	9.2%	65%	35%	6.0%	5.2%	116%
1946	50 years	10.5%	46%	54%	8.7%	5.3%	164%
1966	30 years	12.3%	30%	70%	9.5%	7.9%	120%
1971	25 years	12.5%	30%	70%	10.7%	9.6%	111%
1976	20 years	13.6%	1%	99%	14.5%	10.4%	140%
1981	15 years	13.8%	-2%	102%	14.9%	13.5%	111%
1986	10 years	12.2%	13%	87%	13.6%	11.9%	114%
1991	5 years	14.7%	7%	93%	15.8%	13.1%	120%

Again, the record of the past half-century provides the most dramatic example. A portfolio that was 46% cash and 54% stocks was no more volatile than a portfolio of all U.S. Government bonds, yet it produced an average annual return that was 64% greater than that produced by the all-bond portfolio.

Some pictorial examples of barbell portfolios appear in the following table. As the basis for evaluating risk-return trade-offs in these several cash-stock portfolios, I have used the foregoing Ibbotson-derived data for the half-century following the end of World War II (1946-1995).

EXAMPLES OF BARBELL PORTFOLIOS

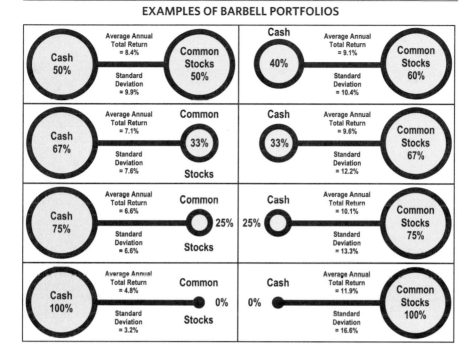

THE TRADITIONAL BARBELL CONCEPT IN BOND INVESTING

The concept of barbell investing with cash and common stocks is borrowed from a common practice in the management of bond portfolios. For bond investors who do not wish to undertake the impossible task of predicting interest rate moves, there are two approaches to designing and maintaining a bond portfolio.

One approach is to "ladder" the maturities of one's bonds. One may start by assembling a portfolio with equal amounts of bonds maturing in each year, one through twenty. Then, each year, as bonds mature, they are rolled over into new twenty-year bonds. With such a program, one has an average ten-year maturity portfolio. Half the bonds mature over the first ten years and half mature over the second ten years.

The second approach is a barbell approach. Here the portfolio consists of half cash and half twenty-year bonds. Again, the average maturity of the portfolio is ten years, but it has two other positive attributes. First, it is more liquid, because half the portfolio is already in cash and so does not need to be converted to cash, if and when cash is needed or desired; and, second, studies similar to this one examining bond portfolios indicate that the average return, over time, is actually higher with the barbell bond portfolio than with the laddered bond portfolio with the same average maturity.

AN INCIDENTAL OBSERVATION REGARDING IMPLEMENTATION

Ironically, it would actually have been easier to have implemented barbell bond portfolios made up of cash and stocks and produced the results previously described than it would have been to implement the U.S. Government bond portfolios and have produced the results indicated with them.

Because they are more volatile, the returns on long-term bonds are greater than the returns on short-term bonds. As a long-term bond approaches maturity, however, it becomes a short-term bond. When it is very close to maturity, its return is no greater than the return on cash. The foregoing models for bonds, then, assume that one purchases a twenty-year U.S. Government bond (or a portfolio of such bonds) each year, sells all his bonds after one year (at which time they have become 19-year bonds), and replaces them with new 20-year bonds. Such a high degree of turnover in a bond portfolio would, of course, be expensive and so detract considerably from the overall return. Anybody who owns bonds is faced with exactly this dilemma, however — whether to hold the bonds until maturity and so reap the lesser rewards of shorter-term bonds through most of the life of the bonds, or to incur the incremental costs of periodically rolling the shortened, but far-from-matured, bonds over into longer, higher-yielding bonds.

In contrast, the owner of the barbell cash and stock portfolio has no such problem. He may achieve his return on cash by simply holding his cash in a bank savings account, and he can achieve his return on stocks by simply assembling and *holding* a diversified list of common stocks. Neither savings accounts nor common stocks have dates of maturity. Admittedly, he may seek to augment the return on his stock portfolio by buying and selling stocks occasionally, but the foregoing studies are not based upon his actively managing his stock portfolio. Much to the contrary, these results are based upon his buying and *holding* a representative portfolio, without any sales or repurchases, throughout the assumed holding period — whether that period is five years, fifty years, or seventy years. If, by giving the stock sector of his portfolio some tender love and care, he can improve his results, relative to the "buy-and-hold" strategy assumed in using a common stock index as a measure of performance, he should be even further ahead of the game.

THE TRADE-OFF

As acknowledged in an earlier paragraph, all investing involves trade-offs. Do "barbell" bonds offer a free lunch? Our theory says, no. What, then, is that less obvious benefit we forego, relative to a bona fide bond portfolio, when we create a barbell portfolio with both less risk and a greater return?

The answer, of course, is that U.S. Government bonds bestow virtually all their net rewards in the form of periodic interest payments which they disburse to us most religiously every six months. Bonds offer us a built-in plan for systematic cash withdrawals.

In contrast, most of the benefits in common stock investing come in the form of capital appreciation and, if one wants to tap into this capital appreciation income to meet living expenses, he needs to set up his own program of periodic cash withdrawals.

To enjoy the greater returns and/or lesser risks of barbell investing, as opposed to bond investing, one must overcome two psychological hurdles: First, he must ignore the distinction between interest or dividend income and capital appreciation income in measuring the performance of his investments; that is, he must focus solely on "total return" which combines both kinds of income into one number. Second, to the extent that he wants to utilize his assets for living expenses, he must be willing to spend his capital gains income as readily as he spends his interest and dividend income.

History shows us that, by using the barbell approach to asset allocation, whereby a combination of common stocks and cash has been substituted for bonds, one has not had to make sacrifices in either the *reliability* or the *magnitude* of his returns; he has, at most, had only to incur an inconvenience in the way he tapped into these returns. For those willing to subject themselves to this inconvenience, however, the rewards have, indeed, been very great.

CONCLUSION

The purpose of the foregoing discussion has been to reemphasize our conviction that the most successful investing is *simple* investing. In spite of the myriad of investment products and services available, the most suitable and rewarding portfolios for most investors can probably be created simply by blending cash and common stocks to produce a level of overall portfolio volatility as great as, but no greater than, its owner can comfortably tolerate.

In short, we probably need not and, in fact, probably ought not, look any farther than to cash and common stocks for the ingredients out of which to construct our entire investment portfolio. This, then, is the "how and why" of what we call our "barbell" approach to asset allocation.

11

DEFERRED ANNUITIES

Contents

Deferred annuities are of two types: fixed rate and variable.

FIXED RATE ANNUITIES

The major shortcoming of a fixed rate annuity is that it is only as secure as the insurance company that sponsors it. That is because the annuity holder's money is commingled with the other assets of the insurance company. From the point of view of safety, money in a fixed rate annuity is comparable to money in a bank that is not insured by the Federal Deposit Insurance Corporation (FDIC). For this reason alone it may not be prudent for individuals subject to anxiety over the safety of their savings to hold money in a fixed rate deferred annuity. Given the many revelations of the shaky finances of previously revered insurance companies, and the subsequent insolvency of some, the advisability of avoiding this particular kind of risk may be still further indicated.

VARIABLE ANNUITIES

Variable annuities are a different breed of cat. They are insurance contracts invested in mutual fund-type vehicles called "sub-accounts." Though the value of a sub-account fluctuates with the securities market in which it is invested, its viability is not dependent upon the financial health of the sponsoring insurance company. The assets in a sub-account are segregated from the assets of the insurance company, and so even bankruptcy of the insurance company should not affect its integrity.

If one elects a deferred annuity, then, the variable annuity seems the way to go. If one is not comfortable investing in the stock market, he can put his money in a sub-account that invests in bonds; if he wants the utmost in safety in bonds, he can select a U.S. Government bond sub-account; and, if he wants the greater stability of cash-type investments, he can select a money market sub-account. There are many other investment options, and one's annuity money can be allocated among different sub-accounts and re-allocated from time to time.

THE IRONY OF THE INCOME TAX DEFERRAL

The real purpose of this paper, however, is to demonstrate that the most heavily merchandised feature of deferred annuities — the deferral of taxes on income until the money is withdrawn — when compared to the cost of ownership of the deferred annuity vehicle is, for most holders, a less-than-worthless attribute.

If we purchase a deferred annuity, we pay no income tax on what our money earns until we withdraw the money. When we withdraw the money, we pay a regular income tax on the accrued income but no tax on our original investment. In comparison, if we are invested with an account that is not tax-deferred, we must pay ongoing income and capital gains taxes; the act of withdrawal, however, does not, itself, trigger a tax.

The first downside to variable annuities is their ongoing costs of ownership. To measure these costs we need only compare the rates of return on deferred annuity sub-accounts with the rates of return on the markets in which these sub-accounts are invested.

Variable annuity sub-accounts (and mutual funds) have historically and consistently underperformed the markets in which they invest. This underperformance is attributable, in part, to the various ongoing fees and expenses associated with maintaining the vehicles but, more significantly, to "market impact" costs or concessions in the prices they must accept as a result of the large size of the positions they must trade when they buy or sell.

Though both mutual funds and sub-accounts are charged fees for management and other services that they require in common, and though mutual funds may have some expenses associated with them that sub-accounts do not, there are more significant expenses charged against sub-accounts that mutual funds do not carry. They include an annual mortality and expense risk (M&E) charge of about 1.25% per year and an additional administrative fee of about 0.15% per year to cover costs involved in offering and administering the variable annuity, such as for printing and distributing correspondence.

In any event, the magnitude of the underperformance of deferred variable annuity sub-accounts, relative to the markets in which they were invested, over the ten-year period ending December 31, 1998, appears in the following table:

TABLE I: AVERAGE ANNUAL TOTAL RATES OF RETURN FOR 10 YEARS ENDING DECEMBER 31, 1998

Investment Category	Direct Ownership	via Variable Annuity	Average Annual Shortfall
Cash	6.03%[1]	4.11%[2]	1.92%
Bonds	11.46%[3]	6.41%[4]	5.04%
Stocks	19.21%[5]	14.02%[6]	5.19%
Stocks (Historical)	11.38%[7]	6.19%[8]	5.19%

[1]Solomon Brothers Index of 6-Month CDs [2]Wiesenberger Index of Money Market Variable Annuities [3]Lehman Brothers Index of Long U.S. Government Bonds [4]Wiesenberger Index of All Fixed Income Variable Annuities [5]Standard & Poor's 500 Composite Index [6]Wiesenberger Index of All Equity Variable Annuities [7]Ibbotson Associates Large Company Stock Index for 73-year period 1926-1998 [8]Assuming the same 5.19% shortfall as for the 10-year period.

The fourth investment category has been added in the above table, based on the more conservative assumption that the stock market will not continue to deliver the 19.21% per year return it has averaged over the past ten years. For a more realistic scenario, the stock market's average return over the past 73 years is used, but the same 5.19% shortfall as for the past ten years for variable annuities is assumed. Deferred annuities have not been around for 73 years, and so we do not have the longer-term data on them. It seems reasonable to assume, however, that their level of expenses, and so the 5.19% shortfall, may remain relatively constant over all types of markets.

The magnitude of the variable annuity deferral advantage (or disadvantage) for the individual owner depends upon his income tax bracket — both federal and state. For purposes of illustration, we have tested for combined federal and state income tax rates of 20%, 30%, 40%, and 50%.

The formula for the amount of after-tax dollars we have at some future point in time, if we invest a dollar today in an account that is *not* tax-deferred, is as follows:

$$[1+R(1-T)]^n$$

where R = before-tax rate of return,
T = tax rate, and n = the number of years.

The formula for the amount of after-tax dollars we have at some future point in time, if we invest a dollar today in a tax-deferred variable annuity, is as follows:

$$1+(1-T)[(1+R)^n-1]$$

With the aid of a computer, we have input the data in the table above for the four investment categories and for each of the four tax brackets to determine how long it would be necessary to hold the variable deferred annuity to produce the same after-tax return as investing in the same category without the benefit of the tax deferral. Our findings were as follows:

	Assumed Combined Federal & State Income Tax Rate			
Investment Category	20%	30%	40%	50%
Cash	Never	Never	106 Years	57 Years
Bonds	Never	Never	Never	Never
Stocks	Never	71 Years	22 Years	14 Years
Stocks (Historical)	Never	Never	Never	147 Years

TABLE II: YEARS BEFORE AFTER-TAX RETURN ON DEFERRED ANNUITY
EQUALS AFTER-TAX RETURN ON DIRECT INVESTMENTS

OTHER CONSIDERATIONS

But even the foregoing calculations fail to reveal all of the shortcomings of owning a deferred annuity. In addition, the following factors should be considered.

[1] In the case of common stocks in an account that is not otherwise tax-deferred, the preceding formula for future after-tax dollars makes the unrealistic assumption that all capital gains are realized and taxed in the year accrued. The effect is to understate the probable future after-tax dollars in such an account. If, on average, capital gains are permitted to accrue for more than one year, there is the additional benefit of some *de facto* tax deferral.

[2] In the case of common stocks, with a deferred annuity, all net accrued capital gains are ultimately taxed at ordinary income tax rates when withdrawn. In the case of an account that is not tax-deferred, long-term capital gains historically have usually been taxed at rates less than those on ordinary income. As of this writing, the maximum federal tax on long-term capital gains is 20%, while the maximum federal tax on ordinary income is 39.6%. Though Uncle Sam says we can defer the tax on our gains in a deferred annuity, he also says that, when we do pay the tax, we must pay at up to double the rate.

[3] If we withdraw the funds from a deferred annuity before reaching age 59½, in addition to our regular income tax, we also pay a 10% penalty tax.

[4] If one accrues his capital gains in a tax-deferred annuity, his heirs forego the step-up in basis that would have been available, had unrealized capital gains accrued in a fully-taxable account. Since most people who have been in the stock market for a reasonable length of time usually die with enormous unrealized gains, this windfall of tax forgiveness is extremely valuable from an estate planning perspective. It is voluntarily cast away with the ownership of a deferred annuity.

THE CARDINAL SIN

Of all the inappropriate places one occasionally encounters a deferred annuity, surely the most blatant is in another tax-sheltered vehicle such as an IRA or a 401(k). There can be little justification for accepting all of the disadvantages of a deferred annuity under circumstances where its primary perceived benefit cannot even be enjoyed. Since one's IRA or 401(k) is already tax-sheltered, there are no incremental tax savings to be realized by funding such an account with a tax-deferred investment.

As an example, it is also not considered an enlightened investment practice to purchase tax-free municipal bonds in either a tax-deferred account such as a traditional IRA or 401(k) or in a tax-exempt account such as a Roth IRA or the portfolio of a charitable institution. There is no logic to accepting the lower rates of return associated with tax-free municipal bonds in accounts where the tax-advantage is redundant.

TO SELL OR TO HOLD A DEFERRED ANNUITY

One way of quantifying the decision of whether to sell or hold a deferred annuity is to relate the incremental return one would expect to earn outside the annuity to the incremental costs of surrendering it.

Deferred annuities commonly have "back-end" loads. Typically, such a load might amount to 7% initially and decrease by 1% until it reaches 0% at the end of the seventh year. If one has had the annuity for two years, and needs to wait another five years to eliminate the charge, he should recognize that, to make up the charge, he need earn only 1% more per year for five years. If we expect to outperform the deferred annuity by 5% per year, as it is indicated in Table I above that we might, we have 4% per year to spare.

Similarly, if we are age 49½ and so faced with a 10% penalty tax for early withdrawal, we really need increase our annual rate of return by 1% per year, at most, between ages 49½ and 59½ to make up the tax. If our expected incremental return is 5% per year, we have a sizable cushion. Remember, the penalty tax and other taxes are assessed upon only the accrued income, not upon the entire value of the annuity.

CONCLUSION

Though the deferral of taxes is tempting, it should be remembered that neither the *deferral* of taxes nor even the *elimination* of taxes is a logical investment goal in itself. Augmentation of one's after-tax return, however, is a legitimate investment objective; and the data is compelling that deferred annuities are rarely an optimal means toward that end.

The cover story for the February 9, 1998 issue of *Forbes Magazine* discusses deferred annuities in detail. The article is introduced on the cover with the following caption:

Don't be a sucker!
Variable annuities are a lousy investment.

and continues inside with,

The great annuity rip-off

Do you want proof positive that investors are irrational? Sales of variable annuities went up 16% last year, to $85 billion.

A variable annuity is a mutual fund-type account wrapped in a thin veneer of insurance that renders the investment earnings tax-deferred. The tax deferral is just about the only good thing you can say about these investment products. Almost everything else about them is bad: the high — sometimes outlandishly high — costs, the lack of liquidity, the fact that the annuity converts low-taxed capital gains into high-taxed ordinary income. That tax deferral comes at a very high price.

★ ★ ★

Any prospective customer who takes the time to understand annuities runs away screaming. A recent report by consulting firm Cerulli Associates puts the matter as delicately as it can: "Information about variable annuity purchases reveals that they do not appear to be based on educated decisions."

This article, by Carolyn T. Geer, can be found in its entirety on the internet in the *Forbes Magazine* archives at www.forbes.com.

1 2

PORTFOLIO TURNOVER AND COMMON STOCK HOLDING PERIODS

In observing the relative performances of common stock portfolios over the years, it has been my impression that the more successful portfolios have had average turnover rates which, over time, have gravitated to about 25% per year which, in turn, has implied average holding periods for the stocks in the portfolios of about four years. Additionally, it is usually the more recently acquired common stocks in such portfolios that seem more appropriate candidates for sale than stocks that have been in the portfolios for longer periods of time. The purpose of this paper is to try to incorporate some bases in logic for these two empirically inferred (and perhaps counter-intuitive) findings.

Contents

PORTFOLIO TURNOVER DEFINED

Turnover is defined as the ratio of the total of all purchases in a portfolio over some period of time to the average value of the portfolio over that period of time. The Looper formula, as it is commonly known, is expressed as follows:

$$\text{Portfolio Turnover} = \frac{\text{Total Purchases}}{\text{Average Portfolio Value}}$$

The period of time used as a reference is usually one year. If the period for which the computations are made is not one year, the number is usually annualized to facilitate comparisons. The Looper formula may, then, be embellished as follows:

$$\text{Average Annual Portfolio Turnover} = \frac{\text{Total Purchases}}{\text{Average Portfolio Value}} \times \frac{365}{\text{Number of Days in Period}}$$

With increasing precision, "Average Portfolio Value" may be the beginning *or* ending value of the portfolio for the period, the average of the beginning *and* ending values, the average monthly values, the average weekly values, or the average daily values.

The turnover figure calculated is also far more meaningful if the period covered is several years, rather than just several months. In fact, if the period is too short, the turnover figure will be meaningless. As an example, if somebody creates a common stock portfolio by investing the proceeds of a maturing certificate of deposit in common stocks and decides to measure his portfolio turnover with the foregoing formula after one week of ownership, he will come up with an Average Portfolio Turnover of 5,214%, indicating that he buys and sells all the stocks in his portfolio 52 times a year when, in fact, it may be his intention never to sell any of the stocks he has just purchased.

CALCULATION OF AVERAGE HOLDING PERIOD

The concept of "average holding period" is perhaps more easily visualized than "average turnover rate." Average holding period tells us, on average, how long after the portfolio manager purchases a security, he sells it. Fortunately, given either average turnover rate or average holding period, one can calculate the other. Given average turnover rate, the formula for average holding period is as follows:

$$\text{Average Holding Period (in Months)} = \frac{12 \text{ Months}}{\text{Average Annual Turnover Rate}}$$

Various turnover rates, then, generate average holding periods as follows:

AVERAGE ANNUAL TURNOVER RATE	AVERAGE HOLDING PERIOD
5%	20 years
10%	10 years
25%	4 years
50%	2 years
75%	16 months
100%	12 months
150%	8 months
200%	6 months
300%	4 months
400%	3 months
600%	2 months

IMPLIED AVERAGE TURNOVER RATES AND AVERAGE HOLDING PERIODS

There are two major difficulties encountered in trying to calculate turnover rates and holding periods from historical purchase and sale and portfolio evaluation data. The first involves adjustments for major inflows of cash into the portfolio or outflows from the portfolio. If the inflows and/or outflows are of significant size and/or frequency, the mathematics become unwieldy. The second difficulty involves the ability to preserve, retrieve, and incorporate into the calculations all the relevant historical portfolio transactions, even if there have been no major cash inflows or outflows.

Fortunately, there is an alternative for estimating these two portfolio characteristics which depends solely upon a static analysis of the portfolio at any given point in time. If one asks the computer to provide a weighted average holding period of all the securities in a portfolio, one has half the battle fought. As long as the portfolio data base includes the date of purchase of each security in it, using amounts owned and current prices, an implied average annual holding period is easily computed. Given the average annual holding period, calculation of the average turnover rate is quite a simple matter, as follows:

$$\text{Average Turnover Rate (in Years)} = \frac{365}{\text{Weighted Average Holding Period (in Days)}}$$

As alluded to above, using this method, or any other method, a recently created or drastically modified portfolio may not begin to reveal its normal average turnover rate and normal average holding period until the passage of a time interval equal, at least, to whatever that average holding period happens to be.

UNACCEPTABLE RATES OF PORTFOLIO TURNOVER

I find the subject of portfolio turnover an interesting one, in part because of the broad spectrum of numbers among stock market strategists as to what "optimum" turnover might be. Let us, however, begin with what it is pretty much universally accepted optimum turnover is not.

"Churning" is the word used to describe excessive trading, sometimes encouraged by a security salesman to generate excessive commissions. Churning, by definition, then, is a level of portfolio turnover which, at least from the point of view of the portfolio owner, is decidedly greater than optimal. I find the subject of "churning" particularly amusing because of the extremely high rates frequently practiced and also because of the extremely high rates frequently construed as acceptable in courts of law and arbitration proceedings.

Generally, a turnover rate of six times per year (holding each of the securities in a portfolio, on average, for only two months) is regarded as prima facie evidence of churning. A turnover rate of 2½ times per year (an average holding period of 4.8 months) is apt to be the threshold of the definition of churning in an arbitration proceeding.

Back in the 1960s, a writer in the *Harvard Law Review* ranked turnover rates, based on the Looper calculation, in what has become known as the "2-4-6" formula. This often-used rule-of-thumb is defined as follows:

AVERAGE TURNOVER	AVERAGE HOLDING PERIOD	DEGREE OF INDICATION OF EXCESSIVE TURNOVER
200%	6 months	Inferential
400%	3 months	Presumptive
600%	2 months	Conclusive

A series of classic court cases covering the four decades following World War II has also indicated a general acceptance of surprisingly high rates of portfolio turnover. As seen in the tabulation below, in fifteen cases in which the turnover rates were construed as *excessive*, the average holding period ranged from as short a period as four days to as long a period as sixteen months, with an average of one month and a median of four months. Similarly, in the seven cases in which the turnover rate was deemed *acceptable*, the average holding period ranged from as long as fifteen months to as short as two weeks, with an average of two months and a median of six months.

EXCESSIVE RATES OF PORTFOLIO TURNOVER					
Year	Turnover	Avg Holding Period	Year	Turnover	Avg Holding Period
1947	150%	8.0 months	1980	200%	6.0 months
1962	158%	7.6 months	1982	600%	2.0 months
1964	293%	4.1 months	1984	667%	1.8 months
1965	327%	3.7 months	1984	2,600%	2.0 weeks
1965	8,939%	4.1 days	1985	893%	1.3 months
1968	143%	8.4 months	1985	1,202%	1.0 month
1968	200%	6.0 months			
1969	77%	15.6 months	Average	1,106%	1.1 month
1970	143%	8.4 months	Median	293%	4.1 months

ACCEPTABLE RATES OF PORTFOLIO TURNOVER		
Year	Turnover	Avg Holding Period
1953	2,500%	2.1 weeks
1975	338%	3.6 months
1976	80%	15.0 months
1977	700%	1.7 months
1978	185%	6.5 months
1984	187%	6.4 months
1987	200%	6.0 months
Average	599%	2.0 months
Median	200%	6.0 months

TURNOVER RATES AMONG INSTITUTIONAL INVESTORS

The average turnover rates among the nation's professionally managed pension funds is said to be about 70%, indicating an average holding period of 17 months. Because mutual funds operate in a fish bowl, because there are so many of them, and because their operations are so exhaustively studied, however, it is probably these institutional investors that provide the best sampling of the level of trading activity among the nation's professionally managed institutional portfolios.

In this regard, in 1998, the 435 mutual funds categorized by Morningstar as "Large-cap Growth" funds had an average turnover of 93% (a 12.9-month average holding period), the 195 funds categorized as "Mid-cap Growth" had an average turnover of 108% (an 11.1-month holding period), and the 183 funds categorized as "Small-cap Growth" had an average turnover of 120% (a 10-month holding period). Over the ten-year period 1989-1998, the "large-cap growth" funds had average turnover rates of 93% (12.9 months), and both the mid-cap and small-cap growth funds had average turnover rates of 114% (10.5 months).

Of equal fascination is the extraordinary rates of turnover of the more active mutual funds. The twenty-five most active growth funds covered by Morningstar in 1998 had portfolio turnover rates that ranged from 215% to 972% and averaged 320%, which rates translate into average holding periods of 24 weeks, 5 weeks, and 16 weeks, respectively

Incidentally, it is, to a large extent, the high turnover rates characteristic of mutual funds that is responsible for their annual total returns' averaging significantly less than benchmark indices used to measure the performances of the particular market sectors in which they invest. High turnover rates exacerbate the problem, unique to large institutional investors such as mutual funds, known as "market impact costs" — the costs, over and above the usual operating expenses and marketing (12b-1) fees, associated with the sacrifices in price that must be incurred when trading large blocks of stock.

TURNOVER RATES IN MUTUAL FUND BOND PORTFOLIOS

Though our primary interest here is the management of common stock portfolios, my most stunning discovery in researching for this paper was the extraordinarily high rates of turnover that prevail in the portfolios of mutual funds that invest solely in high-quality bonds.

Traditional investing assumes that high-quality bonds are purchased to be held to maturity, in which case the turnover in such a bond portfolio should be quite minimal. If we buy equal amounts of bonds each year with maturities of five years and hold them to maturity, our average rate of turnover will be 20%; if we buy ten-year maturities, our turnover rate will be 10%; and, if we buy twenty-year maturities, our turnover rate will be 5%.

Overwhelmingly, the prime determinants of the value of high-quality bond portfolios are changes in the level and structure of interest rates. Therefore, in the case of a high-quality bond portfolio, the only justification for active management is the belief that the portfolio manager can forecast changes in interest rates, and buy and sell bonds in accordance with his forecasts, with enough reliability to outperform a "buy-and-hold strategy" and by a margin great enough more than to cover the cost of retaining his services. (Junk bond portfolios might be expected to be more actively managed than high-quality bond portfolios, since changes in the fortunes of the underlying company impact the *safety* of a junk bond. In such a case a change in the *quality* of the bond, as well as changes in interest rates, may be a major determinant of changes in its value.)

The performance data on actively managed high-quality bond portfolios is not encouraging, however. The following tabulation is insightful:

	LONG-TERM HIGH-QUALITY CORPORATE BONDS	LONG-TERM U.S. GOVERNMENT & AGENCY BONDS
1998		
Number of Funds in Composite	55	33
Average Turnover	163%	168%
Average Holding Period	7.4 months	6.1 months
Operating Expenses (Expense Ratio)	1.06%	1.10%
Total Return Shortfall Relative to Index	-5.37%	-3.49%
1989–1998		
Number of Funds in Composite	18 in 1989 to 55 in 1998	19 in 1989 to 33 in 1998
Average Turnover	139%	170%
Average Holding Period	8.6 months	7.0 months
Average Annual Operating Expenses	1.00% per year	0.89% per year
Average Total Return Shortfall Relative to Index	-2.24% per year	-1.78% per year

For corporate bonds the benchmark index is the Lehman Brothers Corporate Bond Index. For U.S. Government bonds, the benchmark index is the Lehman Brothers Long-Term Government/Corporate Bond Index. The performance of an index is generally accepted as the equivalent of the performance of a randomly selected and unmanaged portfolio of the securities in the particular market sector being measured. It is, therefore, the equivalent of a "buy-and-hold" investment strategy.

Remarkably, mutual funds that invest in high-quality bonds, on average, are actually more actively traded than are mutual funds that invest in common stocks.

As seen in the foregoing data, the significant amounts by which the *underperformance* of high-quality mutual fund bond portfolios exceeds their average annual operating expenses is clear proof that the return on their high rates of activity is *negative*.

IS THERE PROBABLY AN OPTIMUM RATE OF PORTFOLIO TURNOVER?

Other than my own, I am aware of no empirical studies designed specifically to determine *optimum* rates of portfolio turnover. Furthermore, I would be reluctant to subject my own studies to tests of scientific rigor. In fact, based upon my own observations alone, I am more comfortable calling my conclusion that the magic number is 25% (implying an optimum average holding period of 4 years), more of a "hunch" than a demonstrable fact.

Before trying to defend these 25% and 4-year figures, however, let us examine the proposition that there may even be any validity to the concept of an "optimum" rate of portfolio turnover or "optimum" average holding period for a common stock.

Let us assume that there is a publicly traded company scheduled to report its earnings tomorrow and that it is generally accepted, as a near certainty, that the company will announce an earnings increase of 50%. Should we purchase that stock today with the expectation of being able to sell it tomorrow at a profit brought about by the actual announcement of the 50% increase in earnings? Intuitively, we all know that this would not be a good reason for buying the stock. But *why* would it not be a good reason for buying the stock?

The explanation lies in the foregoing phrase "generally accepted." It is "generally accepted" that earnings will be up 50%. Everybody who has inquired believes earnings are going to be up 50%. Hence, the 50% earnings increase is already factored into the price of the stock. To put it into more technical jargon, the price of the stock today already "discounts" the earnings increase to be announced tomorrow. There will be no more profit left to be made in the stock tomorrow as a result of the earnings announcement. The stock has already risen to reflect tomorrow's inevitable earnings announcement.

If *we* know about the big earnings increase to be announced tomorrow, but nobody else knows about it, we have a different situation. We can probably buy the stock (or, still better, buy call options on the stock) today and sell to-morrow and make an enormous profit. In such a case, however, we are "in-siders" with "nonpublic information" and so, if we do act on such information, we must also consider going to jail as one of the likely outcomes.

Let us next consider a company which we have studied with great care and conclude that, because of some unique product or service it provides, it should increase its sales and profits a hundred-fold over the next ten or twenty years, in which case the price of the stock had also ought to go up a hundred-fold over that period of time. We believe it will be another Microsoft or Wal-Mart. Why should we not sell all of our other financial assets and mortgage our house and put every last dime we can dig up into this promis-ing company?

Again, our intuition, if not our experience, tells us that the time frame is too long to ensure accuracy in our prediction. We know that we can use Microsoft and Wal-Mart as examples only with the benefit of hindsight. When those companies were in their infancies, their prospects looked no better than did those of hundreds of other companies much like them. To have been confident of purchasing a Microsoft or a Wal-Mart in their infancies we would have had to purchase ninety-nine other companies that looked just like them at the same time, but which subsequently did not make the grade. With only one one-hundredth of our investment in the big winners, our overall results over the ten- or twenty-year period would have only mirrored the "aggressive growth" stock sector of the stock market, even though Microsoft and/or Wal-Mart were included among our holdings.

Clearly, if the period of time over which we predict is too short (days), the effects we predict are already incorporated, or discounted, in the price of the stock, and so we cannot make above-average profits by acting upon those predictions, even though our predictions are quite accurate. Similarly, if the period of time over which we predict is too long (decades), the competi-tive dynamics and uncertainties of capitalism make such predictions extremely unreliable, and so we cannot make above-average profits by acting upon those predictions either.

The implication would seem to be that, if there is some reasonable or op-timum average period over which judgments about individual common stock can be made, it is a period so long as to be measured in units longer than days, but also a period *not* so long as to be measured in decades. To describe this period of time, let us coin the phrase "Optimum Period of Prediction."

WHAT MIGHT BE THE LENGTH OF THE "OPTIMUM PERIOD OF PREDICTION" IN THE MANAGEMENT OF A COMMON STOCK PORTFOLIO?

In reviewing the literature of common stock, portfolio, and market analyses, one is bound to be impressed by the frequency with which four-year cycles and four-year time horizons are encountered.

Though the divergences have been very wide, the stock market itself is said to have a "natural" cycle of 48 months. The business cycle, too, over very long periods of time, has averaged just about four years. What the Federal Reserve Bank does in controlling the money supply appears to have a lag time of four years before its impact is felt on the rate of inflation. These four-year cycles are frequently regarded as being influenced by the four-year presidential election cycle.

Many analysts use three-to-five year periods (the mid-point of which, of course, is four years) over which they attempt to project a company's earnings. Value Line, in particular, uses time frames of three-to-five years in making its longer term projections. Value Line has further demonstrated that its composites of three-to-five year appreciation potentials for individual stocks has been amazingly reliable in predicting major moves in the stock market as a whole, four years later.

THE THEORY OF CHAOS

The most compelling studies that I have encountered in support of 25% turnover rates and 4-year holding periods have been conducted by a mathematician by the name of Edgar E. Peters. In addition to being a student of mathematics, Peters is a classically trained economist who studied under Nobel Laureate Harry Markowitz, the father of modern portfolio theory. Peters has published two books — *Chaos and Order in Capital Markets* and *Fractal Market Analysis: Applying Chaos Theory to Investment & Economics* — not surprisingly, melding his interests in mathematics with the world of investing.

Not only does the word "chaos" appear in the titles of both of Peters' books, but the concept of chaos underlies his theories of the way the securities markets behave. For this reason, let us grapple with the term "chaos" herewith. The philosopher George Santayana defines chaos as "any order that produces confusion in our minds." As mathematicians define chaos, mental confusion may be an outcome, but it is not its essence. A more technical definition says that chaos is:

a deterministic nonlinear dynamic system, with fractal characteristics and a sensitive dependence on initial conditions,
that can produce random-looking results.

In an effort to impart meaning to such jargon, let us talk about it in
terms of the stock market. In fact, let us talk about it in terms of the hypothetical analysis of a single stock.

In a "deterministic dynamical system," given perfect knowledge of the
initial conditions, the future is perfectly predictable. It is the famous mathematician, Pierre Laplace, to whom is generally attributed original exposition
of the doctrine that, given precise knowledge of the initial conditions, it
should be possible to predict the future of the entire universe.

Presumably, if we have perfect knowledge about the current status of
Company A and its common stock — which includes perfect knowledge
about all the factors that will affect the company and its stock, both internally
and externally, and the relationships among those factors — we can know
all we need to know to predict the future of Company A, including the future
price of its common stock. We can create a mathematical model whereby we
input the initial conditions (our company analysis), and our model identifies
the state of our company at any future time we specify.

The characteristics of a dynamical system that make it "chaotic" are the
presence of a "large set" of initial conditions which are highly "unstable" and
the system's "sensitive dependence upon" these initial conditions. The terms
"large set" and "unstable" would seem to describe appropriately the number
and character of the variables we would encounter if we were to try to list all
of the factors, both internal and external, that completely describe Company
A, its operating environment, and the price of its stock, as we study it today.

It has been suggested that the concept of "sensitivity to initial conditions" may be understood by imagining a boulder precariously perched on
the top of a hill. The slightest push will cause the boulder to roll down one
side of the hill or the other. The subsequent behavior of the boulder depends
upon its sensitivity to the direction of a push — the magnitude of which
push may be quite small. If we are located at the bottom of one side of the
hill, we are keenly interested in which direction the boulder will be pushed.
In a chaotic deterministic dynamical system, all, most, many, or at least
some of the initial conditions are like boulders precariously perched on the
tops of hills.

A system of chaos is often described as a non-linear system. The difference between a linear system and a non-linear system is that a non-linear system relates the variables on either side of the equation with powers other than one. Probably the simplest illustration comes from our high school algebra and geometry. As seen in the following table, the relationship between the circumference of a circle and its radius is linear. The relationship between the area of a circle and its radius is non-linear, however, because the radius of the circle must be squared (carried to the 2nd power) to get the area. Similarly, the relationship between the volume of a sphere and its radius is non-linear because the radius of the sphere must be cubed (carried to the 3rd power) to get its volume.

Variable	Formula	Actual	UNDERESTIMATE		OVERESTIMATE	
			Estimated	% Error	Estimated	% Error
Radius	$r =$	10.00 in.	9.00 in.	-10%	11.00 in.	+10%
Circumference of Circle	$2\pi r =$	62.83 in.	56.55 in.	-10%	69.12 in.	+10%
Area of Circle	$\pi r^2 =$	314.16 sq. in.	254.47 sq. in.	-19%	380.13 sq. in.	+21%
Volume of Sphere	$\frac{4}{3}\pi r^3 =$	4,188.79 cu. in.	3,053.64 cu. in.	-27%	5,575.29 cu. in.	+33%

Notice, also, in the foregoing table that, if we make a 10% error in measuring the radius of a circle, we shall have a 10% error when we calculate its circumference. This is a linear relationship. If we try to measure the area of a circle with a 10% error in our measurement of its radius, however, we end up with an error of 19% to 21% in the area. And, if we try to measure the volume of a cube with a 10% error in our measurement of its radius, we come up with an error of 27% to 33% in our volume.

It is, then, this non-linearity of so much of the real world that makes it so hard to construct mathematical models with which to predict with a very high degree of accuracy. Imagine the price of the stock of our Company A related to hundreds or thousands of variables by powers far in excess of one, two, or three.

The way mathematical chaos manifests itself is by the observation that, no matter how precisely we measure the initial conditions in a system (study the company), our prediction of its subsequent behavior can go radically wrong after a short period of time. Errors in our initial measurements compound themselves over time at an "exponential" rate; or, put another way, the horizon of predictability of such a system grows "logarithmically" with the precision of measurement. What the latter means is that, while we may increase the precision of our initial measurements (our company analysis) by *ten*-fold, the reliability of our predictions may increase at some much lesser rate — by only *two*-fold, for example.

In spite of the fact that there appear to be so many complex relationships that determine the nature of the world around us, the predictive sciences are not all lost causes. As we watch weather forecasters try to predict the path of a hurricane through the Caribbean and into the Gulf of Mexico or up the East Coast, we appreciate how much more confident they are about their predictions for the coming day than they are about their predictions for the coming week.

Depending upon the complexity of what we are trying to predict and the use to which we want to put our predictions, there is probably some time frame over which our predictions can be put to good use, even in chaotic systems.

Though our everyday use of the term might suggest otherwise, mathematical chaos is definitely not complete disorder. It is a level of disorder whereby predictions may be made with some degree of reliability, though not over the very long-term. This would appear to be the explanation of the apparent utility of price and earnings "momentum" stock market strategies that work over shorter periods of time, but not for the long-term.

Chaos theory seems to govern stock market investing somewhat as it governs the growth of an oak tree. We can plant an acorn with a high degree of confidence that an oak tree will grow, but we still have little idea of exactly what the oak tree ultimately will look like. With respect to the volatility of the stock market, chaos theory explains why we might be correct about *what* will happen in the future, without having the foggiest idea of *when* it will happen or *how severe* the happening will be. Major events, like stock market crashes, can be expected, but they cannot be predicted.

What mathematical chaos, as applied to the analysis of common stocks, seems to do for us is provide a conceptual framework for accepting the notion that, though we have some chance of predicting the behavior of individual common stocks over some limited periods of time, we have virtually no chance of making such predictions reliably over very long periods of time. Though individual common stocks may appear to behave in a random fashion over very long periods, they may exhibit discernible patterns over shorter periods.

Mathematical chaos is not an attribute of common stock investing alone. It has application to most of the world's more complex natural phenomena. Systems of chaos are used to describe the nature of biological evolution; they are used in chemistry, physics, medicine, engineering, economics, and even in forecasting the weather. An American meteorologist, Edward Lorenz, in attempting to replicate a calculation in his studies of the weather, discovered that simply rounding his initial conditions to three decimal places rapidly led to widely divergent results. He concluded, therefrom, what has become a classic analogy called the "butterfly effect": the mere flapping of a butterfly's wings in Brazil, Lorenz said, may set off a tornado in Texas.

In his book, *Chaos: Making a New Science,* James Gleick writes, "The most passionate advocates of the new science go so far as to say that twentieth century science will be remembered for just three things: relativity, quantum mechanics, and chaos." Each of these sciences is primarily interested in understanding reality at a characteristic scale: quantum mechanics works at subatomic dimensions; relativity, at the galactic scale where speeds approach the upper limit of light; and chaos theory, at the scale of everyday life.

FRACTALS

Useful to the understanding of the theory of chaos and its application to the stock market is an understanding of "fractals."

A fractal is an object, a system, or a process for which the parts are in some way related to the whole; that is, the individual components are said to be "self-referential" or "self-similar." An example is the branching network in a tree. While each branch and each successive smaller branch is different, all the branches are qualitatively similar to the structure of the tree as a whole.

The science of fractals is frequently illustrated with what are known as "geometric" fractals, the best-known of which are the "Koch Snowflake" and the "Sierpinski Triangle." Let us examine each:

The Koch Snowflake appears on the following page. It is constructed according to the following rules: (a) Construct an equilateral triangle. (b) Add three new triangles, extending outward, with the middle third of each side of the first triangle as the base of each new triangle. (c) Continue, indefinitely, to add new equilateral triangles to the middle third of each side of each new triangle, extending outward in the same way.

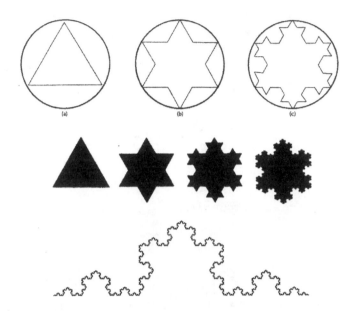

If we continue with the reiterative process described above long enough, we eventually come up with a snowflake-like object, a magnified portion of which appears as the last of the above illustrations. Incidentally, though this process may be repeated an infinite number of times, no part of the snowflake's perimeter ever falls outside a circle drawn through the three vertices of the original triangle.

For our purposes here, the important observations are that a simple formula is used to describe a process for modifying a simple structure, and this process may be repeated an indefinite number of times to arrive at a much more complex structure. Each subsequent version represents simply a propagation of earlier versions down to a smaller scale. Most important, the instructions for constructing the last infinitesimally small triangle are exactly the same as for constructing the first three triangles in illustration (b) above. The "genetic code" for the entire structure, which eventually consists of an infinite number of infinitesimally short straight lines, is implicit in the code for creating the first three appended triangles. The process, from beginning to end, may be said to demonstrate a "long memory" for its "initial conditions."

The Sierpinski Triangle is constructed as follows: (a) Start with a solid equilateral triangle. (b) Remove an equilateral triangle from the center of the first triangle. (c) Remove equilateral triangles from the remaining triangles. (d) Repeat, indefinitely, removing a triangle from each newly created triangle.

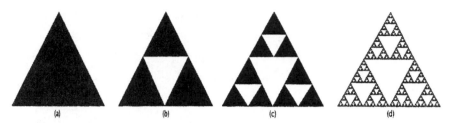

(a) (b) (c) (d)

As with the Koch Snowflake, the Sierpinski Triangle, a complicated structure, is created via the reiteration of a very simple rule; in every stage of the figure's evolution, the basic structure of all the stages that came before is retained — the first stage, and every stage thereafter, contains the blueprint or genetic code for all the stages that follow. Again, the process manifests a "long memory" for its "initial conditions."

The "memories" of geometric fractals remind us of many of the processes we see in nature. The fractal structure and growth of a tree has already been mentioned. The human vascular system, with its complicated assemblage of arteries and veins down to capillaries so small that they will pass no more than a molecule of blood at a time, provide another example. The propagation of a species also illustrates the principle. Presumably, the dominant characteristics of those of us alive today, and those to be born tomorrow, were inherent in the genetic code of our ancestors who lived thousands of years ago. Mother Nature seems to have a very long memory for her initial conditions, irrespective of when we might select "initial" to have been.

Fractal objects, systems, and processes are said to be "different in detail but similar in concept." More technically, they are said to be "locally random, but globally ordered or deterministic."

TIME SERIES AND THE CAPITAL MARKETS

A time series is simply a graph of the behavior of some variable over time. If we plot the average temperature or the range of temperatures for each day for a year, we have a time series. Most stock market charts are time series in that they plot price changes in a stock or a stock market index over some period of time.

Time series fulfill the fractal criteria of being locally random but globally ordered. The randomness of a stock market graph, for example, is described as "noise" and is compared to the static or snow interference we may get with a radio or television transmission. The "signal" or program being transmitted represents the global order.

Because many time series exhibit fractal characteristics, techniques similar to those used to measure the characteristics of geometric fractals are used to measure the fractal characteristics of time series.

The pioneer in this field was a hydrologist by the name of H. E. Hurst. Hurst began working on the Nile River Dam project about 1907 and remained in the Nile region for the next forty or so years. Given widely varying rates of rainfall and water inflow, his problem was to control the discharge rate of the reservoir so that it would neither overflow nor run dry. Hurst developed a technique called "rescaled range analysis" which enabled him to measure the *memory* in a time series, now referred to as the "Hurst exponent." He found that most natural phenomena, including river discharges, temperatures, rainfall, and sunspots, follow a pattern described as a "biased random walk" — a trend with noise.

PETERS' APPLICATION OF CHAOS THEORY TO COMMON STOCK CYCLES

Edgar Peters' contribution has been to extend to the capital markets the rescaled range analysis techniques which Hurst applied to natural phenomena.

It is perhaps useful to begin our summary of the work of Edgar Peters with a definition of the word "cycle" as it us used in the theory of chaos.

We usually think of a cycle, such as the cycle of day and night, as being defined by returns to an initial state (peak-to-peak or trough-to-trough), periodically over identical durations of time. If our daily cycle begins at noon today, it is complete at noon tomorrow, exactly twenty-four hours later. Cycles in the theory of chaos, however, are bound by neither constraint. There need not be a return to an earlier state, nor need a cycle be periodic. A cycle in chaos theory is defined simply as a change in direction. The economy will expand for some indeterminate period, and then it will contract for another unknown period. It will, however, rarely contract exactly to its size before the previous expansion began, nor are business cycles of uniform duration. These expansions and contractions are called cycles, nevertheless. Chaotic cycles are nonperiodic in that their time components cannot be individually determined in advance. A cycle is better visualized here as a "measure of persistence" or the "duration of a trend." In the discussion of the capital markets, a cycle is a "statistical" cycle which measures the length of time over which information impacts a market.

The Hurst exponent can vary between 0.0 and 1.0. 0.5 represents a purely random or utterly unpredictable time series. Hurst exponents of less than 0.5 indicate the presence of what is known as "antipersistent" behavior, while Hurst exponents greater than 0.5 indicate the presence of a long-term memory of previous conditions. Most of the capital markets exhibit Hurst exponents that are greater than 0.5.

With a Hurst exponent greater than 0.5, more recent events have a greater impact than events more distant in time, but the latter still have residual effects. Today's events ripple forward in time like the ripples from a pebble dropped in water. A ripple may persist for quite some time and distance, but it diminishes steadily until, for all intents and purposes, it finally vanishes.

The Hurst model, as applied to the capital markets, implies that, at any given point in time, a set of economic conditions creates a bias in a company's performance, and that this bias persists until the random arrival of some *new* and *significant* information that changes the bias in magnitude, direction, or both.

Using the "rescaled range analysis" technique of chaos theory, and using the Standard & Poor's 500 data covering the 62-year period from 1928 to 1989, as well as the record of the Dow-Jones Industrials for the 102-year period between 1888 and 1990, Peters has demonstrated that the stocks in the U.S. stock market do, indeed, have average cycles of approximately 48 months. What Peters means is that the price of a common stock appears to have a *memory* of its initial conditions that lasts for 48 months. The parameters that define a company's condition today will continue to affect that company for approximately 48 months. The price of the stock will continue to be biased by the dynamics of its initial state for 48 months.

It is also interesting to note, however, that Peters found that certain sectors of the market had different cycles. Cycles for electric utilities extended out to six to seven-and-one-half years. Industrial companies tended to have cycles that averaged somewhat less than 48 months, while high-technology stocks, in particular, had cycles that averaged only eighteen months. Industries characterized by higher rates of innovation appeared to have shorter natural cycles. His findings for some specific companies are summarized on the following page:

STOCK	LONG-TERM MEMORY (MONTHS)
Apple Computer	18
IBM	18
Xerox	18
Coca-Cola	42
McDonald's	42
Anheuser-Busch	48
Niagara Mohawk Power	72
Consolidated Edison	90
Texas State Utilities	90

Another interesting observation that Peters made regarding the behavior of stock market prices is that, if one tries to *measure* memory using increments of time less than 30 days, noise overwhelms signal. The implication is that discussion about a stock's price fluctuations, from day-to-day, or even from week-to-week, is not likely to be meaningful. It is not until after we have a series of data that can be measured in months that we can detect in the data a signal sufficiently strong to be heard over the noise, or seen through the snow, to enable us to make enlightened inferences about a common stock's performance.

AN INTERPRETATION OF NATURAL COMMON STOCK CYCLES AS A GUIDE TO ARRIVING AT OPTIMUM PORTFOLIO TURNOVER RATES

The implication of the above-described phenomena is that the major forces that typically impact industries and companies and the biases that influence the prices of their common stocks tend to persist over periods of time that average four years. It implies that these forces have not only an immediate effect but have a lingering effect as well which lasts, on average, about four years.

It should not be surprising, then, if one observes that the stocks in the most successfully managed portfolios appear to have average holding periods of about four years which, in turn, means average rates of portfolio turnover of the order of 25%.

In fact, for portfolios minimally invested in utilities and/or with an emphasis on higher technology companies, somewhat shorter average holding periods and somewhat higher rates of portfolio turnover are to be expected.

In an article by Robert H. Jeffrey and Robert D. Arnott, in the Spring 1993 issue of the *Journal of Portfolio Management,* I find the following:

> Since any sensible investor understands that a buy-and-hold strategy, if pursued long enough, must inevitably result in flat and eventually negative growth as the holdings mature, portfolios must therefore be pruned, and pruning means turnover, which means realizing gains…[C]onventional wisdom thinks of any turnover in the range of, say, 1% to 25% as categorically low…and of anything greater than 50% as being high…

I have personally come to be quite comfortable with such a perception as a part of my own investment philosophy.

THE LIFO PHENOMENON IN PORTFOLIO MANAGEMENT

LIFO and FIFO are acronyms, respectively, for "Last In, First Out" and "First In, First Out" inventory accounting. It has been my observation that, if one analyzes a portfolio of common stocks in an objective fashion, based upon the fundamentals of the underlying companies, one will conclude that a greater-than-random portion of the common stocks more recently acquired will appear to be more logical candidates for sale than those common stocks held in the portfolio for longer periods of time. In other words, LIFO seems to describe typical portfolio turnover better than FIFO.

Whether via intuition or the application of chaos theory, one might expect companies held for longer periods of time to have more likely matured, or to have encountered problems not foreseen at the time of original purchase, than companies more recently acquired. In fact, if the time between the recommendation to purchase a stock and the recommendation to sell it is too short, there is an understandable implication that the one making the original recommendation did not do his homework well.

In a taxable account, the bias toward selling more recently acquired stocks is easier to understand. Stocks held for a long time are more apt to have large capital gains by virtue of the passage of time alone, and so a large tax cost associated with their sale. Stocks recently acquired, on the other hand, have had less time to accrue significant gains and so are less apt to have significant adverse tax consequences if sold. Furthermore, if a stock is sold at a *loss* in a taxable account, Uncle Sam will subsidize the sale. In short, in a taxable account, given a group of stocks for which the quality, prospects, and position sizes are all considered equivalent, the least attractive candidate for sale will be the issue with the highest percentage gain, while the most attractive candidate for sale will be the issue with the biggest percentage loss. The odds are very great that the stocks with the lower percentage gains or larger percentage losses will have been more recently acquired than the stocks with the larger percentage gains. Tax considerations, then, do explain much of the LIFO turnover bias in a taxable account.

Nevertheless, even in nontaxable accounts — IRAs, pension accounts, and charitable organizations — the LIFO phenomenon still prevails. An objective review of such an account will still usually show that the least desirable holdings are biased toward the issues more recently acquired. This is a paradox.

BUY, HOLD & SELL CATEGORIES

To help understand this LIFO phenomenon in portfolio management, it is useful to recognize that most portfolio managers put securities into one of three categories: (1) "buys" — issues so attractive that their purchase is indicated, if they are not already owned; (2) "holds" — issues not attractive enough to buy, but attractive enough to retain, if currently owned; and (3) "sells" — issues deemed so unattractive as to warrant their disposal.

The LIFO phenomenon is a paradox because the expected evolution of a common stock in a portfolio is from a "buy," to a "hold," to a "sell." At any given time, most of the issues in a portfolio will be classified as "holds."

The difference between a company classified as a "hold" and a company classified as a "buy" is that, while the former is enjoying moderate growth, the latter is in a more *innovative*, and dynamic, and, so, *fragile* stage of growth. Key words here are "innovative" and "fragile."

For example, while we may continue to hold a company that is showing earnings growth of 5% to 10% per year, we are apt to require earnings growth of 10% to 20%, or more, before we consider a company a candidate for purchase. The faster growing company is probably currently more innovative and participating in a market that is changing more dynamically and certainly one that is attracting more competition. Because such a company's endeavors are characterized by higher risk, it is more apt to experience a severe relative reversal of fortunes than is a company plugging along at the slower rate of growth. In short, the faster-growing company we recently acquired is more apt to have stumbled and so surfaced as a "mistake" than is the slower-growth company we had simply continued to hold.

In an effort to make this concept more vivid, imagine that today we review a four-stock portfolio and conclude that two companies should be held and two should be sold and replaced by two others. The two that should be sold are no longer growing. The two that are to be held are growing at 10% per year, while the two we want to buy are growing at 20% per year.

Though we will not know it until after the fact, the two stocks to be held, from this point forward, will have an average future life in the portfolio of four years. One will have three years and the other will have five years. The two new stocks we acquire will also have an average life in the portfolio of four years; but, in this case, one will be one year and the other will be seven years. If we review the portfolio one year hence, it will, therefore, be the one of the two stocks acquired just one year previous that will be the candidate for sale.

Though each pair of stocks — the two "holds" that are growing at 10% per year, and the two "buys" that are growing at 20% per year — have average future life expectancies in the portfolio of four years, the "dispersion" around that average is greater for the faster growing companies. In other words, with respect to the individual companies, our expectations are apt to be wider from the mark with the fast-growing companies than with the slower growing companies. We may be as apt to err on the low side as on the high side, but our potential for error is decidedly greater with the faster growing companies.

Furthermore, in terms of the "Hurst exponents" and memory cycles discussed above, a company in an innovative stage of its evolution is apt to have a shorter memory for current conditions than a less innovative company, or even the same company in a less innovative stage of its development. In other words, our "buys," because they represent companies in more innovative periods of their development, may be expected to have shorter memories for the current conditions under which they are bought than other companies in the portfolio currently classified as "holds."

CONCLUSION

In summary, it appears to me that the most successful common stock portfolios, after the passage of several years following their creation or restructuring, have turnover rates that average about 25% per year, implying average holding periods for the individual stocks in such portfolios of about four years.

Taxable portfolios with large unrealized capital gains may have average turnover rates of somewhat less than 25%, while nontaxable portfolios and portfolios emphasizing more dynamically growing companies in industries characterized by higher rates of innovation may have average turnover rates somewhat in excess of 25%.

Though these concepts of holding periods and turnover rates are useful in the aggregate, when dealing with an entire portfolio over an extended period of time, they are relatively useless concepts when examining a single common stock or a single transaction. Just as one would learn little about an airline's record of delayed departures by examining the data on just one flight, it is necessary to examine the average turnover rate and average holding period for an entire portfolio over some reasonable period of time before conclusions can be drawn as to whether the portfolio is being neglected or is unduly active. As long as such limitations are recognized, however, data on portfolio turnover and average holding periods can be useful guides to portfolio management.

Finally, it should be expected that more recently acquired stocks are more apt to be candidates for early sale, not only because of tax considerations in a taxable account, but also because of the greater vulnerability of companies to severe reversals of fortune when they are enjoying periods of especially innovative and dynamic growth, as is more apt to be the case at the time of purchase and shortly thereafter.

1 3

CONCLUSION

As the result of the observations and research that resulted in the writing and compilation of the twelve chapters of this book, as well as other papers, some of which can be found on our web site at www.dow.us, we have formulated an investment philosophy in which we strongly believe and which we would like to share with our readers in the paragraphs below:

With respect to the management of investment portfolios, we believe the following:

SOME BASIC PRINCIPLES

1 The most important principle upon which to premise an investment philosophy is recognition of the fact that "there is no free lunch." All investing involves trade-offs. For every perceived reward, there is some associated risk — whether perceived or not. Hence, it is incumbent upon every investor, tempted by the potential rewards of any investment, to ascertain the nature and magnitude of the risks involved. To assume that such risks do not exist, just because they are not readily apparent, may be an invitation to disaster.

2 A common characteristic of most *successful* investments, investment portfolios, and investment programs (as with insurance products and estate plans) is their *simplicity*. An investment product or program that is not easily understood is probably not one that is more desirable, but rather is one for which the risks and costs are merely less *visible* than the benefits.

INVESTMENT OBJECTIVES AND POLICIES

3 There are only three investment objectives capable of being achieved and, so, worthy of pursuit:

> A Staying out of irretrievable trouble — which is most likely to be accomplished by owning high-quality securities and being broadly diversified.

> B Participating in the markets or market sectors appropriate to the individual's investment time horizon and personal tolerance for risk and volatility.

> C Accomplishing the foregoing in as efficient a manner as possible in terms of minimizing taxes and not paying for services which add little or no incremental value to the investment process.

4 High-quality and diversification in an investment portfolio serve a purpose similar to that of fire insurance on a house. We carry fire insurance, not because we "expect" our house to burn down. We carry it because, if we do not have it, and our house does burn down, we may not be able financially to recover from the catastrophe.

Similarly, "high-quality" and "diversification" serve the purpose of "insurance" in an investment portfolio. They provide some degree of protection against an economic, monetary, or market calamity which we cannot foresee and do not expect, and which we might not otherwise withstand, or from which we might not otherwise recover, without the added protection, should such a calamity come to pass.

5 It is useful to draw a distinction between "risk" and "volatility" in the securities markets. If "risk" is defined as the possibility of experiencing a decline in the value of one's investments from which one cannot recover, it should probably be minimized for most people. If "volatility" is defined as the normal fluctuations to which all securities markets are subject, it must be endured, if the rewards bestowed by those markets are to be enjoyed.

6 Investment objectives are meaningfully expressed only in terms of investment time horizon and tolerance for risk and volatility and not in terms of desired return. Everybody desires a maximum return but should expect to earn no more than what the markets in which they are invested bestow.

For most people, the time horizon for their investment portfolio planning probably should be longer than they initially think. The attainment of retirement age is hardly a logical point at which to modify one's investment policy. At the very least, one should plan for a period covering one's life expectancy, and married couples should plan for a period covering their joint life expectancy. The life expectancy of an individual age 65 is 20 years, and the life expectancy of the second to die of a couple, each age 65, is 25 years. If one expects to bequeath a portfolio to one's children and hopes that they will pass it on to subsequent generations, the time horizon for investment planning, for all practical purposes, becomes infinite.

7 A good investment policy is one that never changes with changes in market conditions. An investment policy should change only with a major change in one's investment time horizon and/or a change in one's personal tolerance for risk and volatility, which tolerance, for most people, will probably not change throughout their lifetimes. In other words, a suitably formulated investment policy for a particular investor should probably never change throughout that investor's lifetime.

MARKET TIMING

8 We *participate* in markets; we do not try to *outguess* them. Market timing is a futile activity. The most successful investors, over time, are those who remain 100% invested at all times.

The evidence is overwhelming and incontrovertible that even the highest paid professionals are unable to predict with an accuracy of better than 50% such factors as short-term moves in the market, onsets of recessions or recoveries, changes in the direction of interest rates or foreign exchange rates, or changes in the rates of inflation. Therefore, such considerations should remain irrelevant to both the formulation of an investment strategy and the timing of investments or disinvestments. One should put money in the market when one has it to put, and withdraw it from the market when one wants to use it for something else. There should be no other timing considerations.

9 Because, for all practical purposes, the securities markets are efficient, the concept of employing a "professional money manager" to try to *time* the markets, *rotate* from market to market, or sector to sector, or to *buy* individual securities when they are *undervalued* and to sell them when they are *overpriced* is an exercise in futility. In this sense, there are no such "professional" money managers and, so, paying for such a service is counterproductive, serving only to reduce one's overall total return.

ASSET ALLOCATION

10 Except in cases where prohibited (or with certain trusts where income beneficiary and remainderman interests conflict), investors should utilize the "total return" concept of investing. This means that, for investment selection, performance evaluation, and spending purposes, they should draw little distinction between income derived from interest and dividends and income derived from growth of principal.

11 The differences between historical rates of return among the various asset classes are not random events. They are based upon a fundamental principle of capitalism that, for the system to attract investment capital, the greater the uncertainty of the *timing* of one's rewards, the greater must be the magnitude of those rewards. For this reason, it seems reasonable to extrapolate historical differentials into the future.

SECURITY SELECTION

1 2 A good investment is one that represents the simple direct ownership of man-made, value-added, productive resources (plant, equipment, organization, patents, copyrights, trademarks, franchises, and human talent) as opposed to claims on mere commodities (precious metals, the commodities futures markets) or artificially created and/or leveraged risks (derivative securities such as common stock and interest rate options).

1 3 If, when, and as possible, it is far more efficient to own securities outright, rather than through the mediums of "packaged products" such as mutual funds or deferred annuities.

1 4 Inordinately high current yields on investments are usually reliable indicators of less desirable investments. Extremely high current yields may indicate low-quality and a likelihood that the current yield is unsustainable, a low-likelihood of any significant improvement in future performance, or both.

1 5 *Foreign* investing is best accomplished, and real estate investing is effectively achieved, through the ownership of the common stocks of *domestic*, operating companies. A typical portfolio of high-quality, US companies derives 25% of its sales and profits from overseas operations, and about 25% of U. S. corporate assets consists of real estate. The ownership of foreign securities or real estate investment trusts to participate in these two market sectors is both unnecessary and inefficient.

1 6 Initial public offerings (IPOs) should be avoided. Those that turn out well are generally unavailable or in very limited supply; while those that turn out poorly are generally marketed aggressively because of otherwise inadequate demand. The result is that the investor who participates in the IPO market ends up with little of the former but much of the latter and, so, below-average market performance with IPOs in general.

PORTFOLIO MONITORING

1 7 Except to accommodate a particular income tax or diversification objective, the decision of whether a specific security in a portfolio should be held or sold generally should not be predicated upon the behavior of its "price" while it has been in the portfolio. If the securities markets are "efficient," which for all practical purposes we believe they are, the "current" price is the only "correct" price. The decision to hold or sell should, then, be based upon an assessment of whether or not the *company's* quality and potential for earnings growth continue to conform to the standards established for the portfolio, irrespective of the price of the stock.

1 8 Most high-quality companies that stumble eventually pick themselves up and get back on track again. For such companies, the question of whether to hold or sell becomes one of whether or not one wants to wait out the "turnaround time." If the turnaround time is apt to be too long, it is probably better to trade the stock for one that appears currently to have its act together and to be able to keep it that way for a while.

1 9 Though an important consideration, the tax on a gain, if realized, should not necessarily be a barrier to the sale of that security. Historically, just a randomly selected, unmanaged list of common stocks has accrued capital gains at an average rate of 7.9% per year; for growth portfolios, the rate has been considerably higher. If, on average, one *realizes* gains at a rate *less* than the rate at which one *accrues* gains, securities become "locked in," and it becomes increasingly difficult to adapt the portfolio to the standards of diversification, quality, and potential for growth that optimize the investor's longer-term interests.

PORTFOLIO ADVISORS

2 0 Legitimate roles for a portfolio advisor are the following:

A To help the client view his investment portfolio in the broad context of his overall individual circumstances and aspirations, with special consideration being given to appropriate income tax, retirement, and estate planning objectives.

B To help the client (1) identify an appropriate investment time horizon over which to plan; (2) assess his personal tolerance for risk and volatility; (3) become acquainted with the rates of return historically available with alternative investment policies, and the degree of risk and volatility historically associated with each; and (4) structure a diversified portfolio of securities that conforms to his personal investment time horizon and tolerance for risk and volatility.

C To help the client monitor his portfolio over time to make sure that the individual securities in it continue to conform to the client's standards of quality and potential for growth and that the portfolio as a whole remains reasonably well-diversified.

D To provide the client with a perspective with which to assess his ongoing performance which, for any short period of time, may differ dramatically from expected longer-term results. Though disparagingly referred to as "hand holding," this function is vitally important for most clients, if they are going to continue to be successful investors. On a cruise ship, in the middle of the ocean in a violent storm, even the most experienced traveler, if he is to travel that way again, may need reassurance from the captain that the vessel is not leaking, that the engines are still running, and that the ship is, in fact, still on course.

ABOUT DOW WEALTH MANAGEMENT, LLC

Dow Wealth Management is a private account portfolio manager headquartered in Falmouth, Maine with origins dating to 1937.

Through three generations of Dow family management, the company has provided academically sound, objective investment advice and the highest quality financial services to its clients.